Data on Music Education

Data on Music Education

A national review of statistics describing
education in music and the other arts

Compiled by Daniel V. Steinel

MENC MENC MENC MENC

MUSIC EDUCATORS NATIONAL CONFERENCE

1902 Association Drive, Reston, VA 22091-1597

Printed in the United States of America
ISBN 0-940796-87-2

Contents

Chapter 4: Examinations

CHAPTER 5: Secondary School Offerings and Enrollments

Chapter 6: School District Policies and Practices

Acknowledgments

MENC appreciates the permission for use of copyrighted material granted by the Association for School, College and University Staffing, Inc. and The College Board. Special thanks to Vance Grant of the National Center for Education Statistics (NCES) for his assistance in extracting data for the degrees awarded before 1978 and for sharing his wealth of knowledge about reports available from NCES.

The help of the MENC Publications Department in publishing this collection is gratefully acknowledged. Special thanks to the MENC publications staff and to Sheila Wilson.

Daniel V. Steinel
Information Service Manager

Introduction

Among the duties of the Music Educators National Conference (MENC) Information Service is the collection and dissemination of information about music education. The Information Service distributes information through the "FYI" column in *MENC Soundpost*, through the publication of books, and in short responses to requests. This publication, which is part of the Information Service's ongoing dissemination activity, is an update of *Music and Music Education: Data and Information* (1984), the first publication of the Information Service. While the focus of this publication is on music education, forty of the forty-three tables include an art area other than music or refer to the arts as a group.

Many sources were examined in preparing this book. Only data found to be reliable and relevant to music education were included. Data were considered relevant if they were representative of the United States as a whole and provided either a "snapshot" of the current status or documentation of a trend for some aspect of music education. Data were considered reliable if the organization reporting the data was known to use accepted statistical practices in areas such as sample design and selection and data manipulation and analysis.

The data included were gathered using a variety of techniques, with surveys being the most common. Both sample surveys, which gather data from only a portion of a selected population, and universe surveys, which gather data from all members in a selected population, were used. Most data can be classified as opinions and estimates, self-reported facts, or administrative records. In some cases, all three types of information are available in one area. For example, the chapter on secondary enrollments includes, estimates of district officials, student reported participation in extracurricular activities, and data derived from high school transcripts. Comparing data from the three sources, one finds figures that seem to contradict each other, but each is accurate within its own context.

Most of the data include information that provide a context for the figures; e.g., the data on secondary enrollments include courses other than music. Other more general factors—socioeconomic, educational, and cultural—of life in the United States are also helpful in interpreting the data, but are beyond the scope of this publication. Publications such as *Statistical Abstract of the United States,* published yearly by the United States Department of Commerce's Bureau of the Census, and *Digest of Education Statistics,* published yearly by the United States Department of Education's National Center for Education Statistics, are good sources of such contextual data.

The data contained in this publication are comprehensive within the data selection parameters. In this age of information, one might expect that more data would be available. The lack of additional information reflects the current status of arts education in the United States.

Chapter 1

Employment Rates

Data in this chapter are from a National Endowment for the Arts (NEA) study and two National Center for Education Statistics (NCES) surveys. The NEA data do not include elementary and secondary arts teacher employment rates, and the NCES data include arts education as a nonextractable part of the humanities aggregate. Therefore neither is comprehensive, but each contributes to the complex picture of employment in music education.

1.1 Humanities graduate occupations

Major occupations of 1985–1986 bachelor's-degree recipients in the humanities: 1987

	Major occupation (percentage)								
Job characteristics	**Clerk**	**Educator**	**Business/manager**	**Public affairs/social worker**	**Sales person**	**Writer/artist**	**Laborer**	**Communication**	**Service person**
All graduates	19	12	8	7	7	6	5	4	4
Reporting job related to major	33	71	58	91	34	97	17	88	17
Reporting job had career potential	38	50	64	83	39	67	18	68	12
Reporting job required no degree	78	10	30	45	58	53	92	21	84
Average annual salary	$13,400	$10,800	$17,400	$16,000	$13,200	$14,500	$12,900	$14,600	$10,000

Note: Table includes only occupations in which at least 3 percent of graduates were employed.

Source: U.S. Department of Education, National Center for Education Statistics, 1987 Recent College Graduates Survey. As printed in Porter, Joanell, *Occupational and Educational Outcomes of 1985–86 Bachelor's Degree Recipients* (Washington, DC, National Center for Education Statistics), 1989, p. 25.

Major occupations of 1985–1986 bachelor's-degree recipients in the humanities: 1987

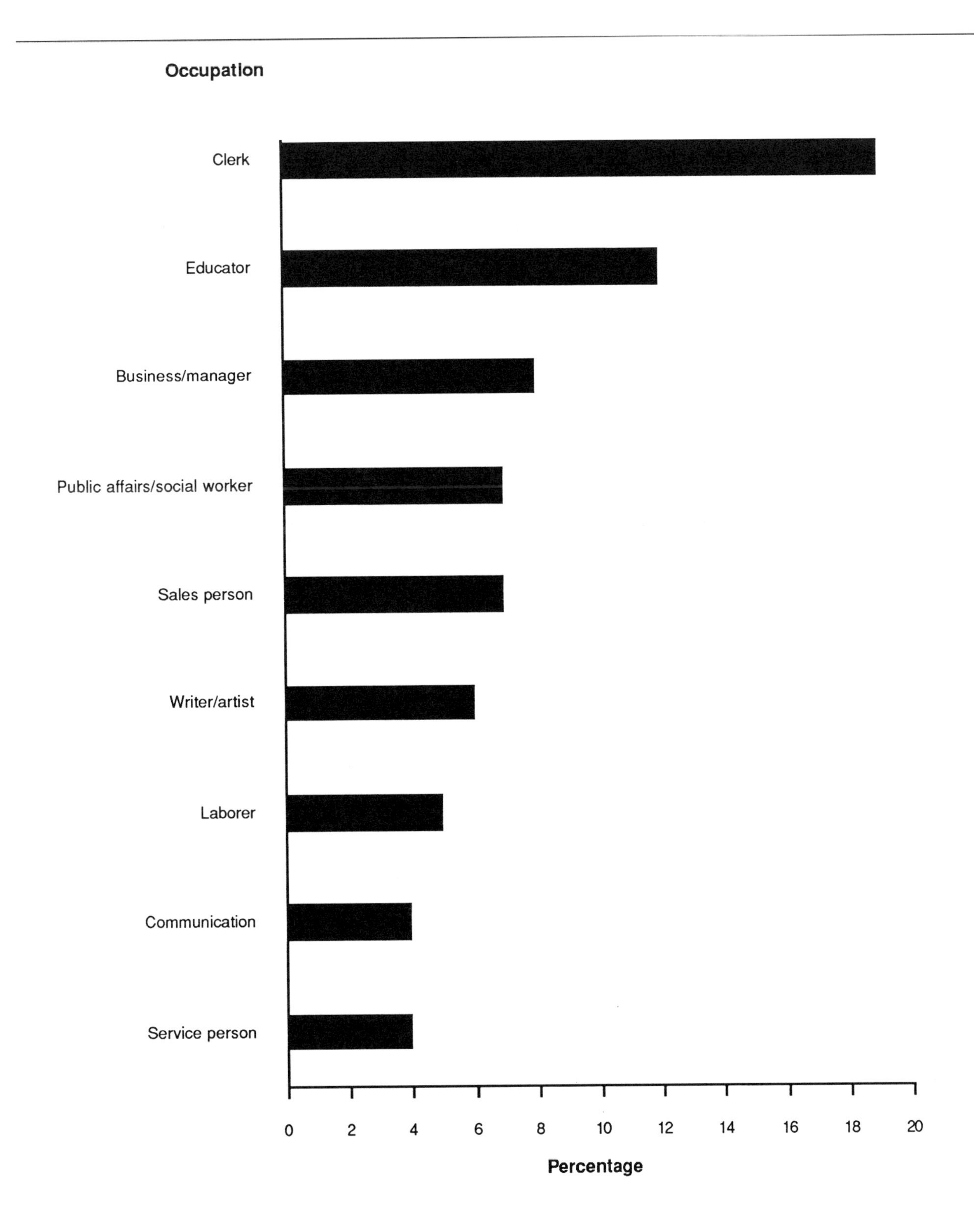

1.2 Employed teachers: Combined elementary/secondary

Teachers* employed in public and private elementary and secondary schools: November 1, 1983

Field of assignment	Total		Public		Private	
	Number	Percentage	Number	Percentage	Number	Percentage
Total	2,553,300	100.0	2,216,200	100.0	337,200	100.0
Preprimary education	89,100	3.5	58,200	2.6	30,900	9.2
General elementary education	873,300	34.2	726,200	32.8	147,100	43.6
Art	**50,700**	**2.0**	**44,100**	**2.0**	**6,700**	**2.0**
Basic skills/remedial education	42,300	1.7	38,500	1.7	3,800	1.1
Bilingual education	29,900	1.2	29,000	1.3	900	0.3
Biological and physical sciences	131,100	5.1	114,700	5.2	16,400	4.9
Biology	28,800	1.1	24,800	1.1	4,000	1.2
Chemistry	14,600	0.6	12,100	0.5	2,500	0.7
Physics	8,700	0.3	7,100	0.3	1,600	0.5
General and all other sciences	78,900	3.1	70,700	3.2	8,200	2.4
Business (nonvocational)	53,800	2.1	48,900	2.2	4,900	1.5
Computer science	9,200	0.4	6,800	0.3	2,400	0.7
English language arts	182,700	7.2	161,900	7.3	20,800	6.2
Foreign languages	50,400	2.0	39,400	1.8	11,000	3.3
Health, physical education	131,500	5.1	117,200	5.3	14,300	4.2
Home economics	38,100	1.5	36,600	1.7	1,500	0.5
Industrial arts	43,700	1.7	42,300	1.9	1,300	0.4
Mathematics	147,100	5.8	128,900	5.8	18,100	5.4
Music	**79,100**	**3.1**	**70,000**	**3.2**	**9,100**	**2.7**
Reading	47,700	1.9	43,400	2.0	4,400	1.3
Social studies/social sciences	142,400	5.6	126,900	5.7	15,400	4.6
Special education	264,100	10.3	250,100	11.3	14,000	4.1
Mentally retarded	54,400	2.1	52,300	2.4	2,100	0.6
Seriously emotionally disturbed	26,800	1.0	22,900	1.0	3,800	1.1
Specific learning disabled	73,200	2.9	70,400	3.2	2,800	0.8
Speech impaired	27,700	1.1	26,900	1.2	800	0.2
Other special education	82,000	3.2	77,500	3.5	4,500	1.3
Vocational education	64,300	2.5	63,700	2.9	600	0.2
Other elementary education	29,800	1.2	27,200	1.2	2,600	0.8
Other secondary education	53,500	2.1	42,500	1.9	11,100	3.3

* In full-time equivalents.

Note: Percentages calculated on unrounded numbers. Because of rounding, details may not add to totals.

Source: Teachers in Elementary and Secondary Education, Historical Report (Washington, DC: U.S. Department of Education Center for Education Statistics), March 1987, p. 10.

Teachers employed in public and private elementary and secondary schools: November 1, 1983

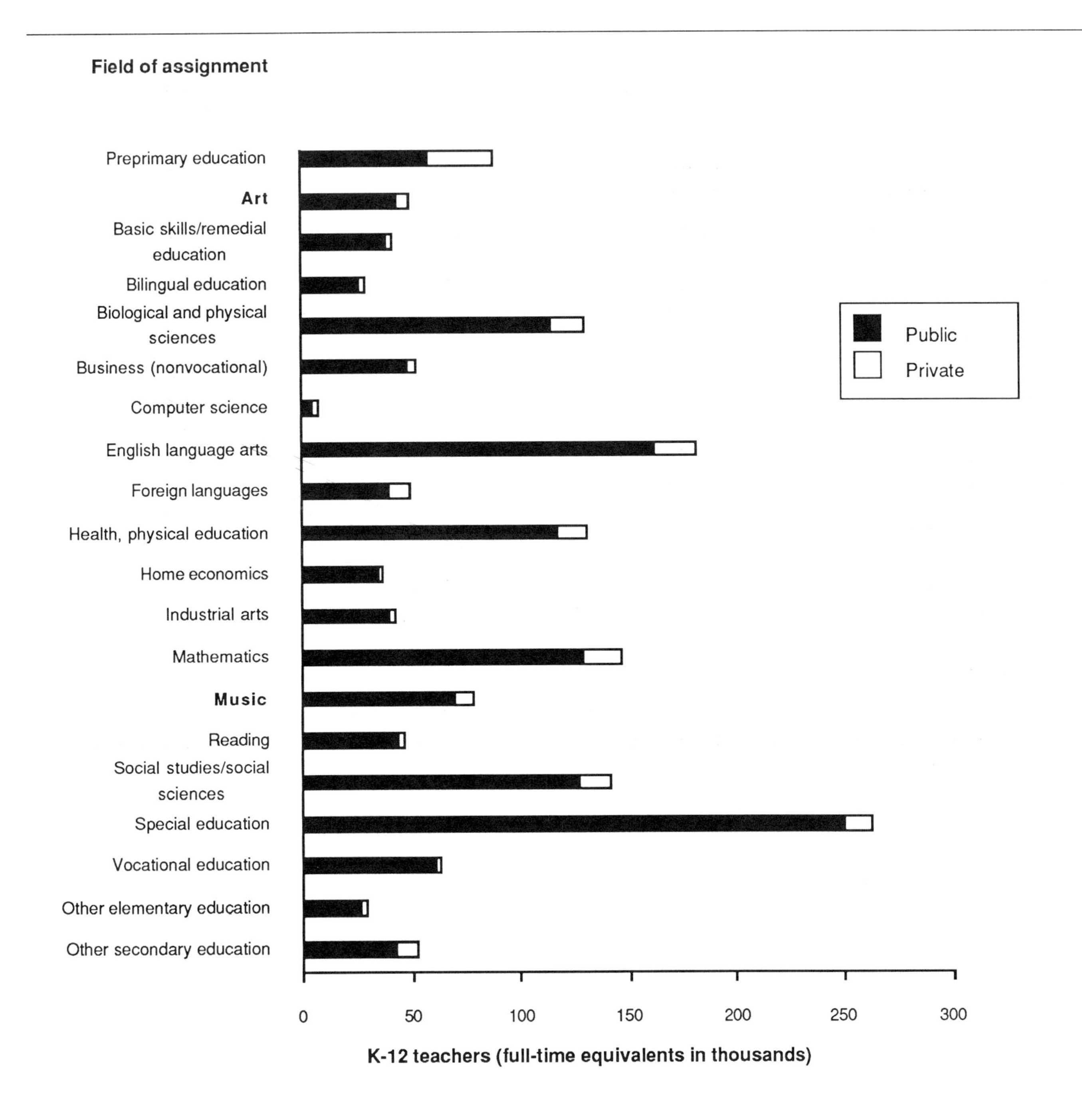

Note: Number of General elementary education teachers not shown due to limitations of chart size.

1.3 Employed teachers: Elementary

Teachers* employed in public and private elementary schools: November 1, 1983

Field of assignment	Total		Public		Private	
	Number	Percentage	Number	Percentage	Number	Percentage
Total elementary	1,428,800	100.0	1,205,500	100.0	223,300	100.0
Preprimary education	89,100	6.2	58,200	4.8	30,900	13.8
General elementary education	873,300	61.1	726,200	60.2	147,100	65.9
Art	**19,600**	**1.4**	**16,700**	**1.4**	**2,800**	**1.3**
Basic skills/remedial education	30,000	2.1	27,300	2.3	2,700	1.2
Bilingual education	25,100	1.8	24,800	2.1	300	0.1
English language arts	23,000	1.6	19,400	1.6	3,600	1.6
Foreign languages	4,100	0.3	2,500	0.2	1,500	0.7
Health, physical education	43,800	3.1	37,700	3.1	6,100	2.7
Home economics	3,700	0.3	3,600	0.3	100	0.0
Industrial arts	3,800	0.3	3,700	0.3	100	0.0
Mathematics	20,800	1.5	17,500	1.5	3,300	1.5
Music	**38,700**	**2.7**	**33,600**	**2.8**	**5,100**	**2.3**
Reading	27,200	1.9	24,600	2.0	2,700	1.2
Science	15,500	1.1	12,700	1.1	2,800	1.3
Social studies/social sciences	16,700	1.2	14,200	1.2	2,500	1.1
Special education	164,900	11.5	155,600	12.9	9,300	4.2
Mentally retarded	32,400	2.3	31,000	2.6	1,400	0.6
Seriously emotionally disturbed	16,400	1.2	14,500	1.2	2,000	0.9
Specific learning disabled	44,000	3.1	42,000	3.5	2,000	0.9
Speech impaired	22,200	1.6	21,400	1.8	800	0.4
Other special education	49,900	3.5	46,700	3.9	3,200	1.4
All other elementary	29,800	2.1	27,200	2.3	2,600	1.2

* In full-time equivalents.

Note: Percentages calculated on unrounded numbers. Because of rounding, details may not add to totals.

Source: Teachers in Elementary and Secondary Education, Historical Report (Washington, DC: U.S. Department of Education Center for Education Statistics), March 1987, p. 11.

Teachers employed in public and private elementary schools: November 1, 1983

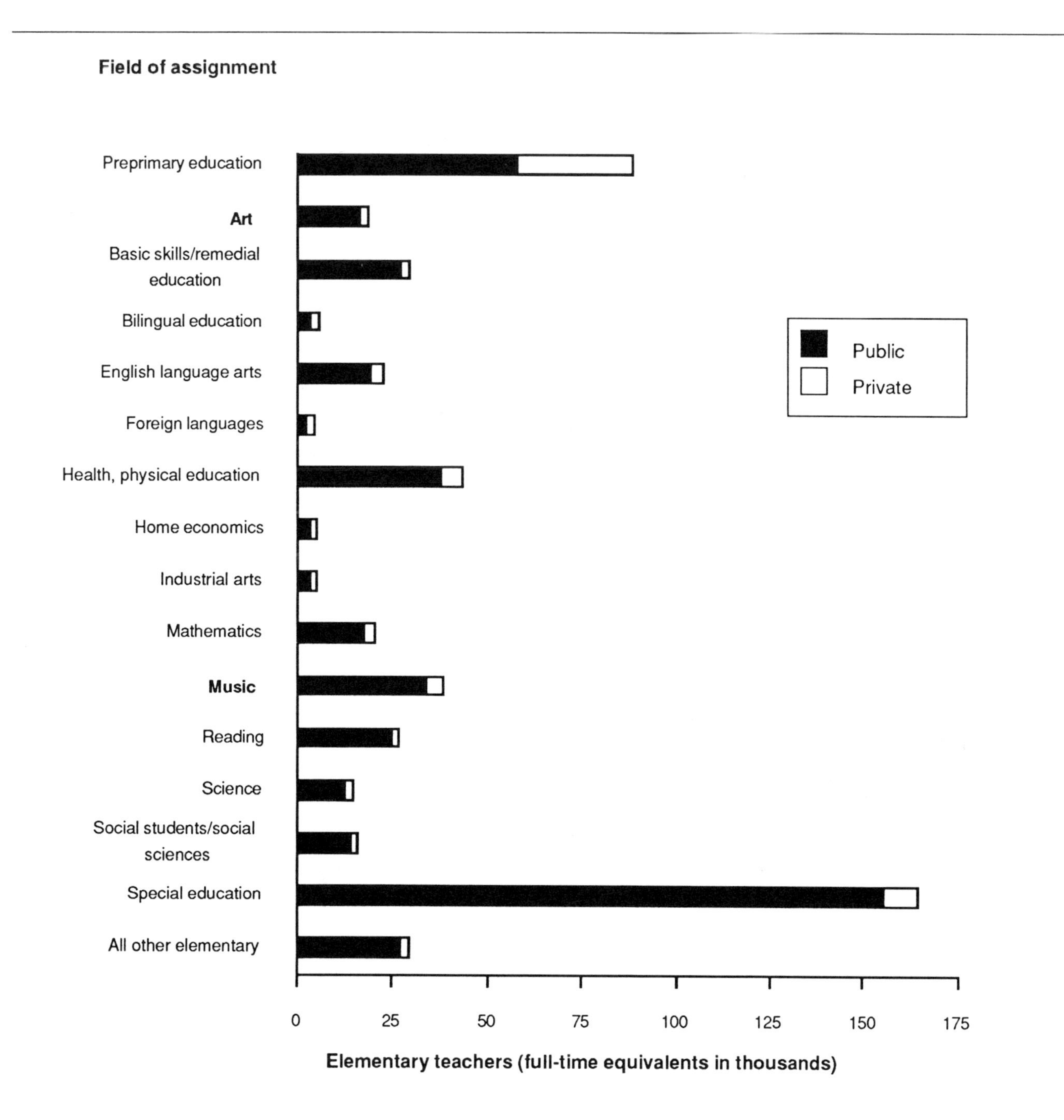

Note: Number of General elementary education teachers not shown due to limitations of chart size.

1.4 Employed teachers: Secondary

Teachers* employed in public and private secondary schools: November 1, 1983

Field of assignment	Total		Public		Private	
	Number	Percentage	Number	Percentage	Number	Percentage
Total secondary	1,124,500	100.0	1,010,700	100.0	113,800	100.0
Art	**31,100**	**2.8**	**27,300**	**2.7**	**3,800**	**3.4**
Basic skills/remedial education	12,300	1.1	11,200	1.1	1,100	1.0
Bilingual education	4,800	0.4	4,200	0.4	600	0.5
Biological and physical sciences	115,600	10.3	102,000	10.1	13,600	11.9
Biology	28,800	2.6	24,800	2.5	4,000	3.5
Chemistry	14,600	1.3	12,100	1.2	2,500	2.2
Physics	8,700	0.8	7,100	0.7	1,600	1.4
General and all other sciences	63,500	5.6	58,000	5.7	5,500	4.8
Business (nonvocational)	53,800	4.8	48,900	4.8	4,900	4.3
Computer science	9,200	0.8	6,800	0.7	2,400	2.1
English language arts	159,700	14.2	142,400	14.1	17,200	15.1
Foreign languages	46,400	4.1	36,900	3.7	9,400	8.3
Health, physical education	87,700	7.8	79,500	7.9	8,200	7.2
Home economics	34,400	3.1	33,000	3.3	1,400	1.3
Industrial arts	39,900	3.5	38,600	3.8	1,300	1.1
Mathematics	126,300	11.2	111,400	11.0	14,800	13.0
Music	**40,400**	**3.6**	**36,400**	**3.6**	**4,000**	**3.5**
Reading	20,500	1.8	18,800	1.9	1,700	1.5
Social studies/social sciences	125,600	11.2	112,700	11.1	13,000	11.4
Special education	99,200	8.8	94,500	9.4	4,700	4.1
Mentally retarded	22,000	2.0	21,400	2.1	600	0.6
Seriously emotionally disturbed	10,300	0.9	8,400	0.8	1,900	1.6
Specific learning disabled	29,200	2.6	28,400	2.8	800	0.7
Speech impaired	5,550	0.5	5,500	0.5	50	0.0
Other special education	32,200	2.9	30,800	3.1	1,300	1.2
Vocational education	64,300	5.7	63,700	6.3	600	0.6
All other secondary	53,500	4.8	42,500	4.2	11,100	9.7

* In full-time equivalents.

Note: Percentages calculated on unrounded numbers. Because of rounding, details may not add to totals.

Source: Teachers in Elementary and Secondary Education, Historical Report (Washington, DC: U.S. Department of Education Center for Education Statistics), March 1987, p. 12.

Teachers employed in public and private secondary schools: November 1, 1983

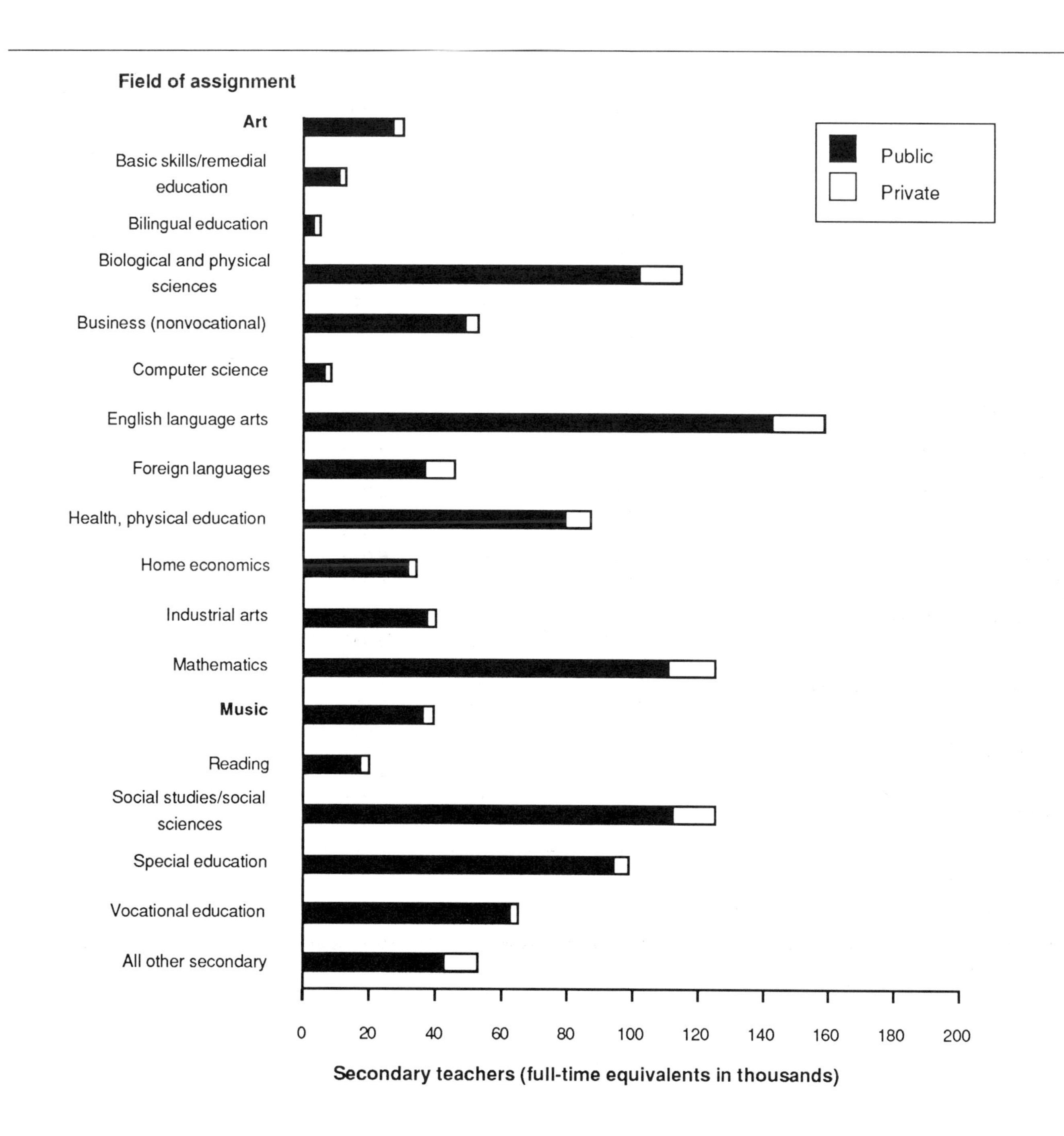

1.5 Uncertified teachers: Combined elementary/secondary

Uncertified teachers* in public and private elementary and secondary schools: November 1, 1983

Field of assignment	Total		Uncertified teachers		Uncertified as percentage of total teachers
	Number	Percentage	Number	Percentage	
Total	2,553,300	100.0	88,260	100.0	3.5
Preprimary education	89,100	3.5	12,370	14.0	13.9
General elementary education	873,300	34.2	21,230	24.1	2.4
Art	**50,700**	**2.0**	**1,590**	**1.8**	**3.1**
Basic skills/remedial education	42,300	1.7	840	0.9	2.0
Bilingual education	29,900	1.2	3,590	4.1	12.0
Biological and physical science	131,100	5.1	5,360	6.1	4.1
Biology	28,800	1.1	1,090	1.2	3.8
Chemistry	14,600	0.6	590	0.7	4.1
Physics	8,700	0.3	490	0.6	5.6
General and all other science	79,000	3.1	3,190	3.6	4.0
Business (nonvocational)	53,800	2.1	990	1.1	1.8
Computer science	9,200	0.4	790	0.9	8.7
English language arts	182,700	7.2	4,560	5.2	2.5
Foreign languages	50,400	2.0	2,830	3.2	5.6
Health, physical education	131,500	5.1	2,920	3.3	2.2
Home economics	38,100	1.5	360	0.4	0.9
Industrial arts	43,700	1.7	620	0.7	1.4
Mathematics	147,100	5.8	6,080	6.9	4.1
Music	**79,100**	**3.1**	**2,390**	**2.7**	**3.0**
Reading	47,700	1.9	1,560	1.8	3.3
Social studies/social sciences	142,400	5.6	3,380	3.8	2.4
Special education	264,100	10.3	9,340	10.6	3.5
Mentally retarded	54,400	2.1	1,800	2.0	3.3
Seriously emotionally disturbed	26,800	1.0	1,250	1.4	4.7
Specific learning disabled	73,200	2.9	3,050	3.5	4.2
Speech impaired	27,700	1.1	400	0.5	1.4
Other special education	82,000	3.2	2,840	3.2	3.5
Vocational education	64,300	2.5	2,350	2.7	3.6
Other elementary education	29,800	1.2	900	1.0	3.0
Other secondary education	53,500	2.1	4,220	4.8	7.9

* In full-time equivalents.

Note: Percentages calculated on unrounded numbers. Because of rounding, details may not add to totals.

Source: Teachers in Elementary and Secondary Education, Historical Report (Washington, DC: U.S. Department of Education Center for Education Statistics), March 1987, p. 16.

Percentage of teachers uncertified per teaching field: November 1, 1983

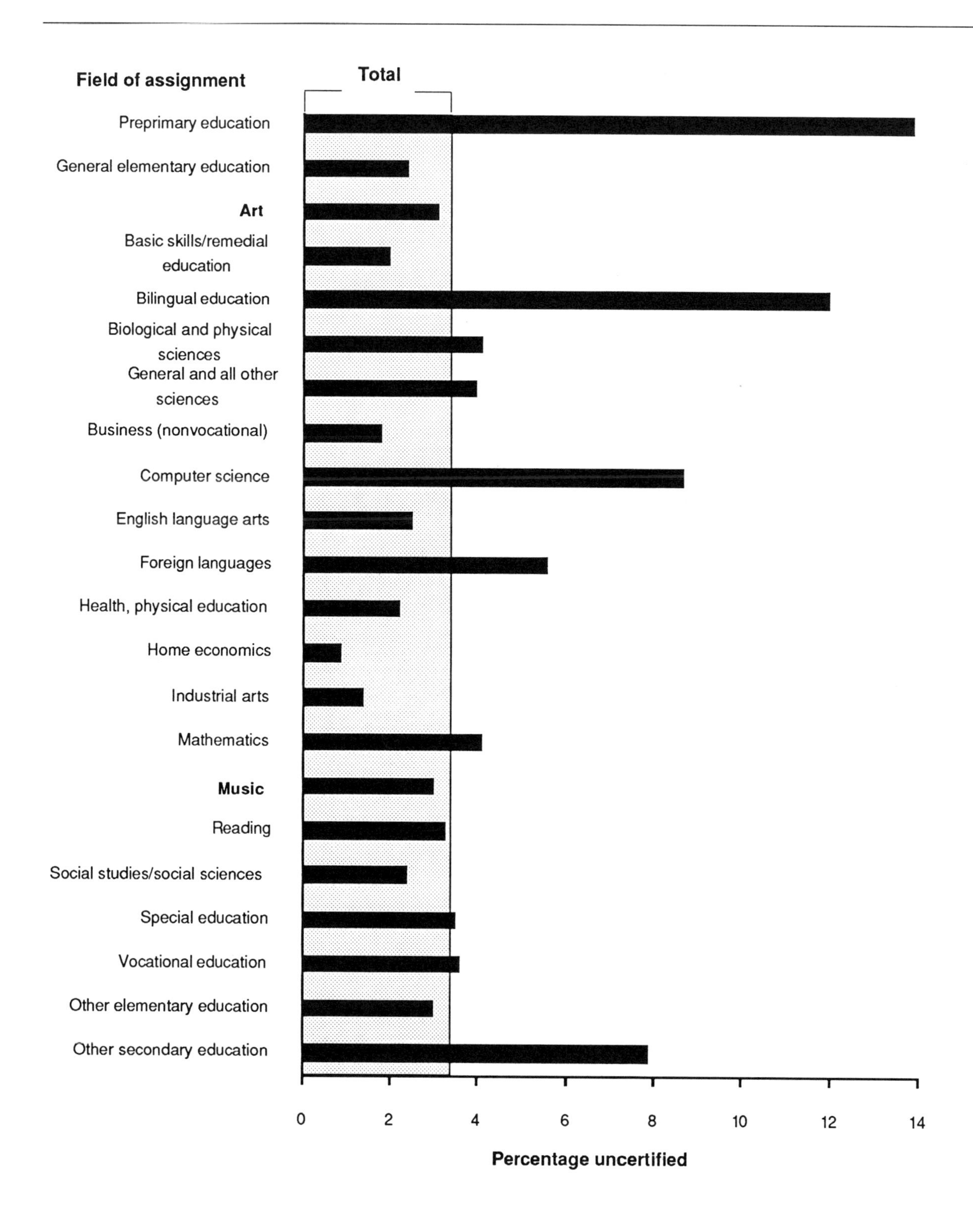

1.6 Uncertified teachers: Elementary

Uncertified teachers* in public and private elementary schools: November 1, 1983

Field of assignment	Total		Uncertified teachers		Uncertified as percentage of total teachers
	Number	Percentage	Number	Percentage	
Total elementary	1,428,800	100.0	51,420	100.0	3.6
Preprimary education	89,100	6.2	12,370	24.1	13.9
General elementary education	873,300	61.1	21,230	41.3	2.4
Art	**19,600**	**1.4**	**720**	**1.4**	**3.7**
Basic skills/remedial education	30,000	2.1	420	0.8	1.4
Bilingual education	25,100	1.8	2,980	5.8	11.9
English language arts	23,000	1.6	670	1.3	2.9
Foreign languages	4,100	0.3	490	0.9	12.0
Health, physical education	43,800	3.1	1,280	2.5	2.9
Home economics	3,700	0.3	40	0.1	1.2
Industrial arts	3,800	0.3	90	0.2	2.3
Mathematics	20,800	1.5	870	1.7	4.2
Music	**38,700**	**2.7**	**1,480**	**2.9**	**3.8**
Reading	27,200	1.9	1,060	2.1	3.9
Science	15,500	1.1	620	1.2	4.0
Social studies/social sciences	16,700	1.2	480	0.9	2.8
Special education	164,900	11.5	5,730	11.2	3.5
Mentally retarded	32,400	2.3	1,180	2.3	3.6
Seriously emotionally disturbed	16,400	1.2	710	1.4	4.3
Specific learning disabled	44,000	3.1	1,720	3.3	3.9
Speech impaired	22,200	1.6	360	0.7	1.6
Other special education	49,900	3.5	1,760	3.4	3.5
All other elementary	29,800	2.1	900	1.8	3.0

* In full-time equivalents.

Note: Percentages calculated on unrounded numbers. Because of rounding, details may not add to totals.

Source: Teachers in Elementary and Secondary Education, Historical Report (Washington, DC: U.S. Department of Education Center for Education Statistics), March 1987, p. 17.

Percentage of elementary teachers uncertified per teaching field: November 1, 1983

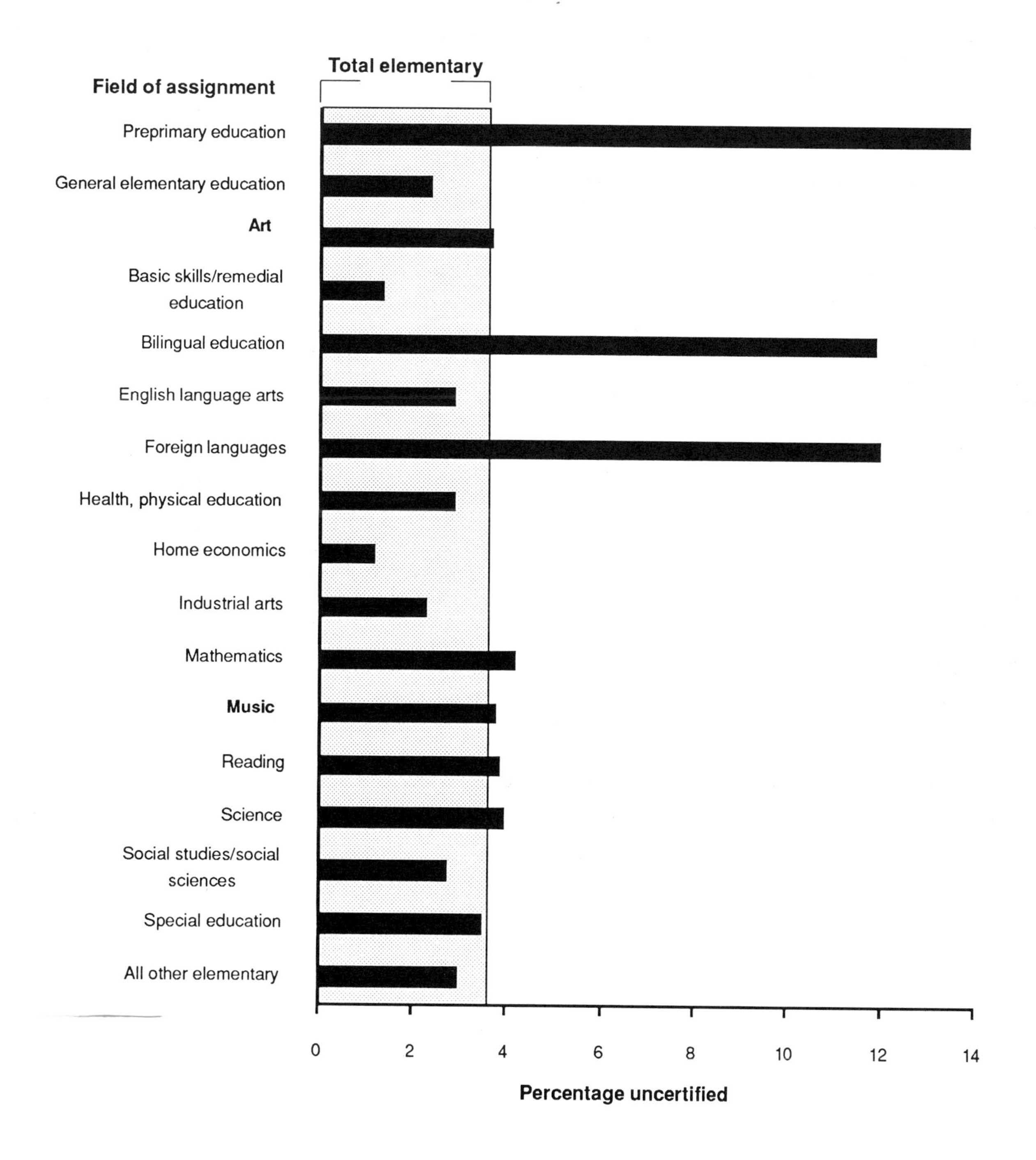

1.7 Uncertified teachers: Secondary

Uncertified teachers* in public and private secondary schools: November 1, 1983

Field of assignment	Total		Uncertified teachers		Uncertified as percentage of total teachers
	Number	Percentage	Number	Percentage	
Total	1,124,500	100.0	36,840	100.0	3.3
Art	**31,100**	**2.8**	**870**	**2.4**	**2.8**
Basic skills/remedial education	12,300	1.1	420	1.1	3.4
Bilingual education	4,800	0.4	610	1.7	12.8
Biological and physical sciences	115,600	10.3	4,730	12.8	4.1
Biology	28,800	2.6	1,090	2.9	3.8
Chemistry	14,600	1.3	590	1.6	4.1
Physics	8,700	0.8	490	1.3	5.6
General and all other sciences	63,500	5.6	2,560	7.0	4.0
Business (nonvocational)	53,800	4.8	990	2.7	1.8
Computer science	9,200	0.8	790	2.1	8.7
English language arts	159,700	14.2	3,890	10.5	2.4
Foreign languages	46,400	4.1	2,340	6.4	5.1
Health, physical education	87,700	7.8	1,640	4.4	1.9
Home economics	34,400	3.1	320	0.9	0.9
Industrial arts	39,900	3.5	540	1.5	1.3
Mathematics	126,300	11.2	5,210	14.2	4.1
Music	**40,400**	**3.6**	**900**	**2.5**	**2.2**
Reading	20,500	1.8	500	1.4	2.4
Social studies/social sciences	125,600	11.2	2,900	7.9	2.3
Special education	99,200	8.8	3,610	9.8	3.6
Mentally retarded	22,000	2.0	620	1.7	2.8
Seriously emotionally disturbed	10,300	0.9	540	1.5	5.2
Specific learning disabled	29,200	2.6	1,330	3.6	4.6
Speech impaired	5,500	0.5	40	0.1	0.7
Other special education	32,200	2.9	1,080	2.9	3.3
Vocational education	64,300	5.7	2,350	6.4	3.6
All other secondary	53,500	4.8	4,220	11.5	7.9

* In full-time equivalents.

Note: Percentages calculated on unrounded numbers. Because of rounding, details may not add to totals.

Source: Teachers in Elementary and Secondary Education, Historical Report (Washington, DC: U.S. Department of Education Center for Education Statistics), March 1987, p. 18.

Percentage of secondary teachers uncertified per teaching field: November 1, 1983

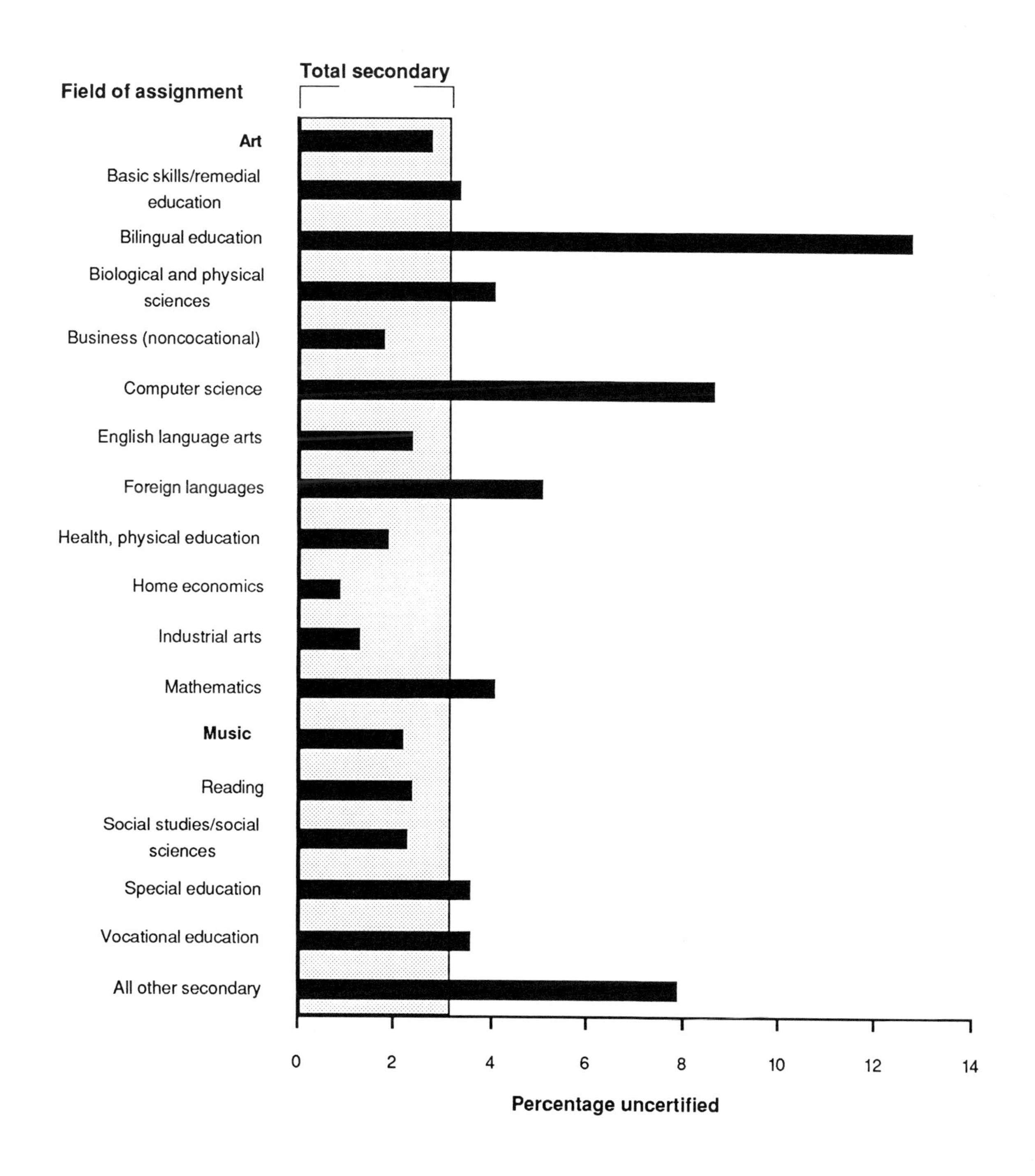

1.8 Artist employment

Artist labor force, employment, and unemployment: 1983–1986 (1980 classification)

Occupation	1983	1984	1985	1986	Change 1983–86	Change 1985–86
Total, all civilian workers	111,550,000	113,544,000	115,462,000	117,834,000	+6,284,000	+2,372,000
Employed	100,834,000	105,005,000	107,150,000	109,597,000	+8,763,000	+2,447,000
Unemployed	10,717,000	8,539,000	8,312,000	8,237,000	-2,480,000	-75,000
Unemployment percentage	9.6	7.5	7.2	7.0	-2.6	-.2
Professional specialty occupation	13,219,000	13,629,000	13,946,000	14,228,000	+1,009,000	+282,000
Employed	12,820,000	13,286,000	13,630,000	13,911,000	+1,091,000	+281,000
Unemployed	399,000	343,000	316,000	317,000	-82,000	+1,000
Unemployment percentage	3.0	2.5	2.3	2.2	-.8	-.1
All artists	1,301,000	1,418,000	1,482,000	1,500,000	+199,000	+18,000
Employed	1,223,000	1,351,000	1,411,000	1,439,000	+216,000	+28,000
Unemployed	78,000	67,000	71,000	61,000	17,000	10,000
Unemployment percentage	6.0	4.7	5.0	4.1	-1.9	-.9
Actors and directors	71,000	78,000	91,000	93,000	+23,000	+2,000
Employed	60,000	68,000	77,000	86,000	+26,000	+9,000
Unemployed	11,000	10,000	14,000	7,000	-4,000	-7,000
Unemployment percentage	15.7	13.3	15.4	7.7	-8.0	-7.7
Announcers	41,000	59,000	54,000	58,000	+17,000	+4,000
Employed	38,000	55,000	51,000	55,000	+17,000	+4,000
Unemployed	3,000	4,000	3,000	3,000	0	0
Unemployment percentage	6.7	6.2	5.3	5.9	-.8	+.6
Architects	108,000	109,000	133,000	135,000	+27,000	+2,000
Employed	103,000	107,000	130,000	132,000	+29,000	+2,000
Unemployed	5,000	2,000	3,000	3,000	-2,000	0
Unemployment percentage	4.3	1.8	2.2	1.9	-2.4	-.3
Authors	64,000	72,000	71,000	77,000	+13,000	+6,000
Employed	62,000	71,000	70,000	75,000	+13,000	+5,000
Unemployed	2,000	1,000	1,000	2,000	0	+1,000
Unemployment percentage	2.5	1.4	1.4	2.6	+.1	+1.2
Dancers	12,000	14,000	17,000	18,000	+6,000	+1,000
Employed	10,000	12,000	15,000	15,000	+5,000	0
Unemployed	a	a	a	a	a	a
Unemployment percentage	a	a	a	a	a	a
Designers	415,000	466,000	504,000	504,000	+89,000	0
Employed	393,000	448,000	484,000	484,000	+91,000	0
Unemployed	22,000	18,000	20,000	20,000	-2,000	0
Unemployment percentage	5.2	3.9	3.9	4.0	-1.2	+.1
Musicians/composers	170,000	174,000	163,000	171,000	+1,000	+8,000
Employed	155,000	161,000	152,000	164,000	+9,000	+12,000
Unemployed	15,000	13,000	11,000	7,000	-8,000	-4,000
Unemployment percentage	8.6	7.3	6.5	3.9	-4.7	-2.6
Painters/sculptors/craft artists/ and artist printmakers	192,000	220,000	207,000	194,000	+2,000	-13,000
Employed	186,000	212,000	200,000	189,000	+3,000	-11,000
Unemployed	6,000	8,000	7,000	5,000	-1,000	-2,000
Unemployment percentage	3.3	3.5	3.2	2.7	-.6	-.5
Photographers	119,000	128,000	134,000	131,000	+12,000	-3,000
Employed	113,000	123,000	129,000	127,000	+14,000	-2,000
Unemployed	6,000	5,000	5,000	4,000	-2,000	-1,000
Unemployment percentage	5.0	3.9	3.5	2.7	-2.3	-.8

Occupation	1983	1984	1985	1986	Change 1983–86	Change 1985–86
Teachers of art, drama, and music (higher ed)	43,000	41,000	42,000	43,000	0	+1,000
Employed	42,000	40,000	41,000	42,000	0	+1,000
Unemployed	1,000	1,000	1,000	1,000	0	0
Unemployment percentage	2.2	2.4	2.4	1.9	-.3	-.5
Other artists[b]	66,000	57,000	66,000	76,000	+10,000	+10,000
Employed	61,000	54,000	62,000	70,000	+9,000	+8,000
Unemployed	5,000	3,000	4,000	6,000	+1,000	+2,000
Unemployment percentage	7.1	5.8	5.6	7.8	+.7	+2.2

[a] Data base is too small for estimate.

[b] Not elsewhere classified.

Note: Data in this table reflect the 1980 revision of occupational categories and are not directly comparable with previous data of this type from the National Endowment for the Arts. All the unemployment percentages shown in the table (with the exception of the rates for All Artists) were calculated by the Bureau of Labor Statistics using unrounded data. Therefore, calculating unemployment rates using the rounded levels for unemployed and labor force shown in the table may yield slightly different rates. See Appendix for methodological note on Current Population Survey.

Source: National Endowment for the Arts, Research Division, "Artist Employment in 1986," Washington, DC, Note 22, March 1987. (Data provided by U.S. Department of Labor, Bureau of Labor Statistics, Current Population Survey, unpublished data.) Reprinted from: Westat, Inc. (under contract to the National Endowment for the Arts), *A Sourcebook of Arts Statistics: 1987*, Rockville, MD, April 1988, p. 92.

1.8a Artist employment

Change in artist unemployment percentage (1983–1986)

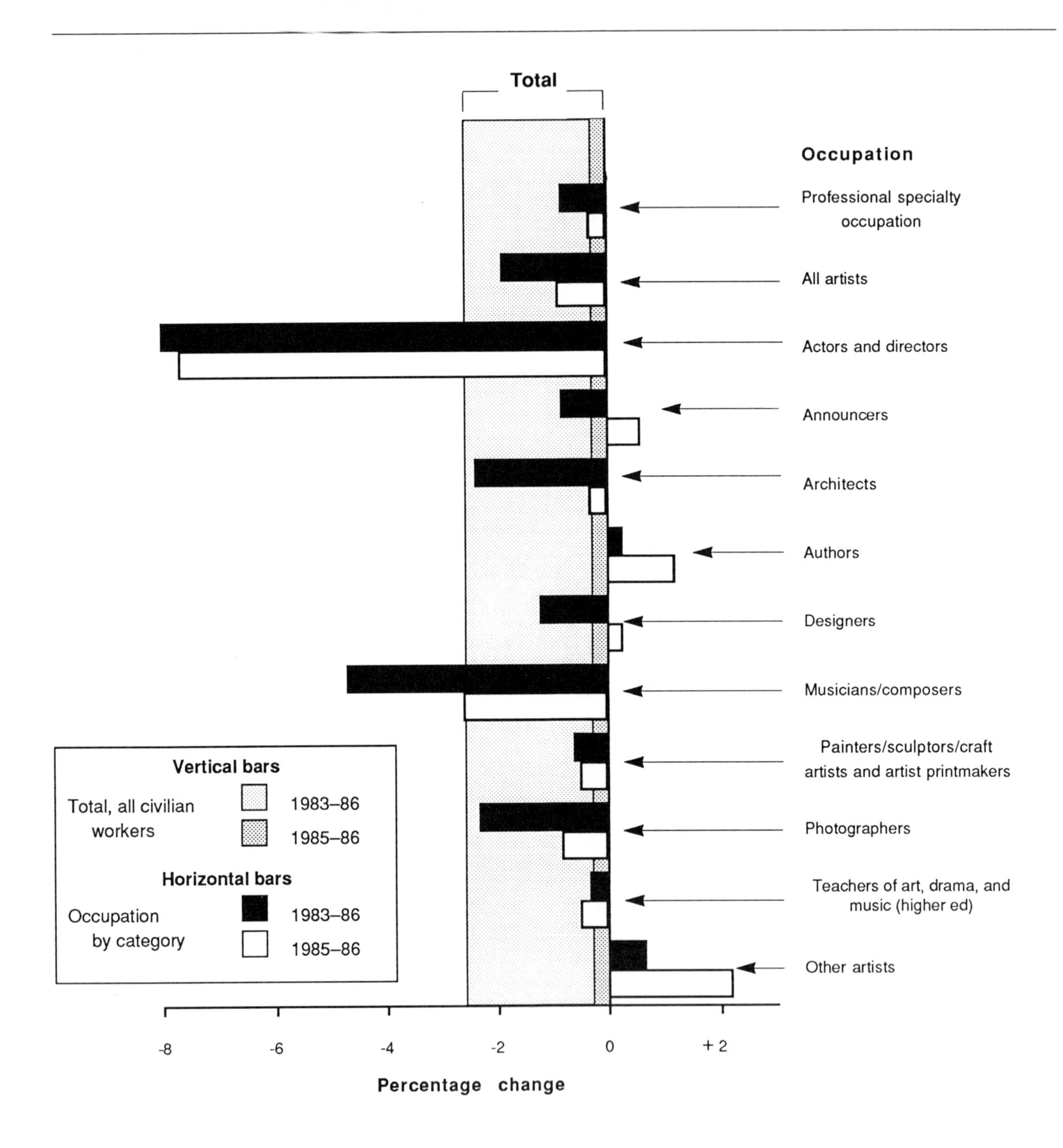

Chapter 2

Employment Opportunities

The first three tables in this chapter report actual shortages: "positions vacant, abolished, or transferred to another field...because a candidate was unable to be found." The remaining tables are based on opinions of college placement officers and district-level school officials.

Of special interest in the first three tables is the fact that the shortages per 1,000 teachers in 1983 in the subject areas of music and art were equal to or greater than shortages in math or science.

2.1 Teacher shortages: Combined elementary/secondary

Teacher candidate shortages* in public and private elementary and secondary schools: November 1, 1983

Field of assignment	Total teachers		Candidate shortages		Shortages per 1,000 teachers
	Number	Percentage	Number	Percentage	
Total	2,553,300	100.0	3,965	100.0	1.6
Preprimary education	89,100	3.5	80	2.0	0.9
General elementary education	873,300	34.2	742	18.7	0.8
Art	**50,700**	**2.0**	**184**	**4.6**	**3.6**
Basic skills/remedial education	42,300	1.7	122	3.1	2.9
Bilingual education	29,900	1.2	263	6.6	8.8
Biological and physical sciences	131,100	5.1	225	5.7	1.7
Biology	28,800	1.1	49	1.2	1.7
Chemistry	14,600	0.6	27	0.7	1.9
Physics	8,700	0.3	39	1.0	4.5
General and all other sciences	79,000	3.1	111	2.8	1.4
Business (nonvocational)	53,800	2.1	20	0.5	0.4
Computer science	9,200	0.4	34	0.9	3.7
English language arts	182,700	7.2	171	4.3	0.9
Foreign languages	50,400	2.0	77	1.9	1.5
Health, physical education	131,500	5.2	99	2.5	0.8
Home economics	38,100	1.5	27	0.7	0.7
Industrial arts	43,700	1.7	82	2.1	1.9
Mathematics	147,100	5.8	263	6.6	1.8
Music	**79,100**	**3.1**	**243**	**6.1**	**3.1**
Reading	47,700	1.9	20	0.5	0.4
Social studies/social sciences	142,400	5.6	67	1.7	0.5
Special education	264,100	10.3	1,027	25.9	3.9
Mentally retarded	54,400	2.1	153	3.9	2.8
Seriously emotionally disturbed	26,800	1.0	99	2.5	3.7
Specific learning disabled	73,200	2.9	190	4.8	2.6
Speech impaired	27,700	1.1	175	4.4	6.3
Other special education	82,000	3.2	408	10.3	5.0
Vocational education	64,300	2.5	68	1.7	1.1
Other elementary education	29,800	1.2	33	0.8	1.1
Other secondary education	53,500	2.1	119	3.0	2.2

* In full-time equivalents.

Note: Percentages calculated on unrounded numbers. Because of rounding, details may not add to totals.

Source: Teachers in Elementary and Secondary Education, Historical Report (Washington, DC: U.S. Department of Education Center for Education Statistics), March 1987, p. 13.

2.1a Teacher shortages: Combined elementary/secondary

Shortage per 1,000 combined elementary and secondary teachers by teaching field: November 1, 1983

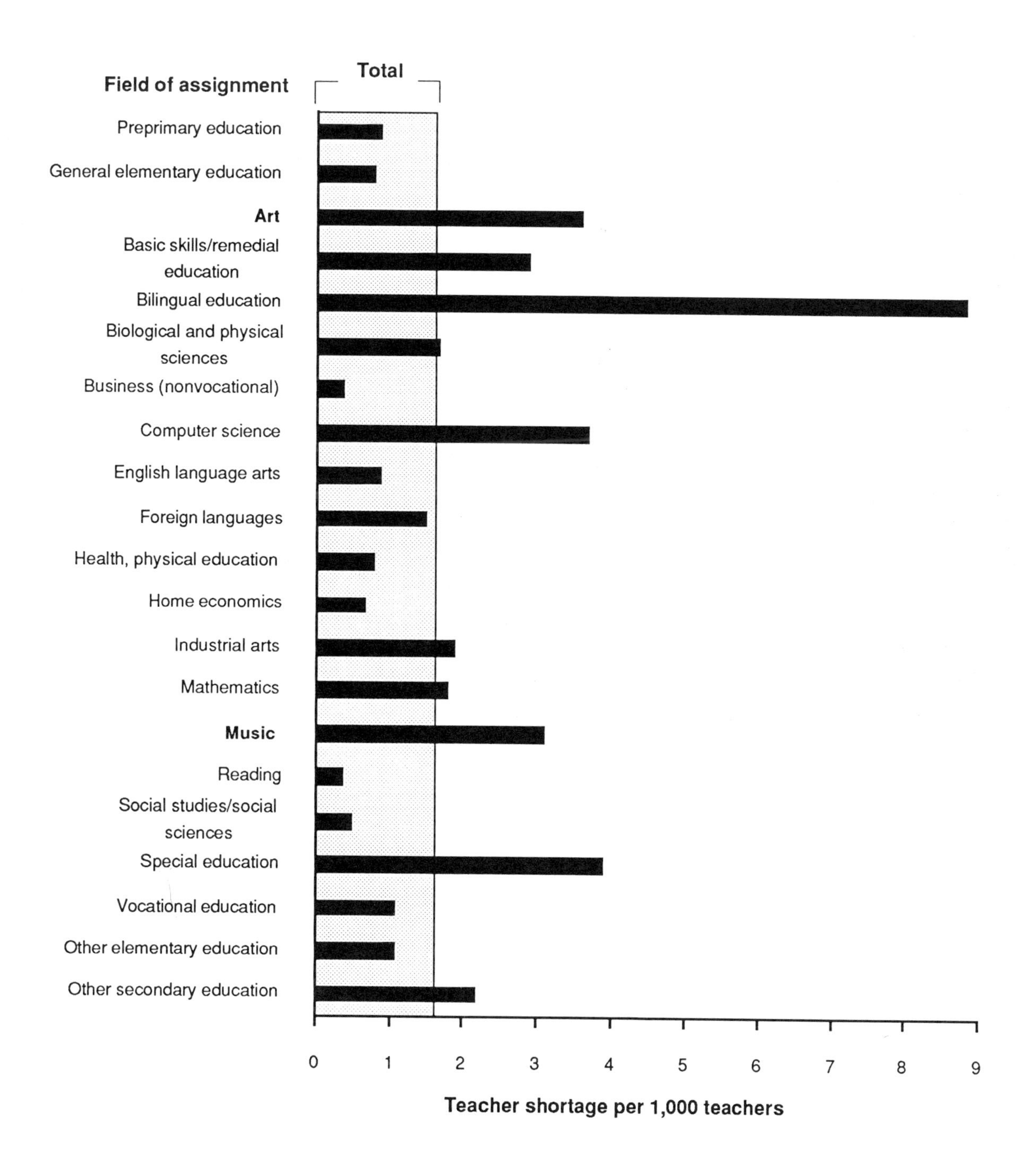

2.2 Teacher shortages: Elementary

Teacher candidate shortages* in public and private elementary schools: November 1, 1983

Field of assignment	Total teachers		Candidate shortages		Shortages per 1,000 teachers
	Number	Percentage	Number	Percentage	
Total elementary	1,428,800	100.0	2,317	100.00	1.6
Preprimary education	89,100	6.2	80	3.5	0.9
General elementary education	873,300	61.1	742	32.0	0.8
Art	**19,600**	**1.4**	**89**	**3.8**	**4.5**
Basic skills/remedial education	30,000	2.1	81	3.5	2.7
Bilingual education	25,100	1.8	245	10.6	9.8
English language arts	23,000	1.6	12	0.5	0.5
Foreign languages	4,100	0.3	4	0.2	1.0
Health, physical education	43,800	3.1	33	1.4	0.8
Home economics	3,700	0.3	1	0.0	0.3
Industrial arts	3,800	0.3	2	0.1	0.5
Mathematics	20,800	1.5	86	3.7	4.1
Music	**38,700**	**2.7**	**159**	**6.9**	**4.1**
Reading	27,200	1.9	3	0.1	0.1
Science	15,500	1.1	61	2.6	3.9
Social studies/social sciences	16,700	1.2	0	0.0	0.0
Special education	164,900	11.5	690	29.8	4.2
Mentally retarded	32,400	2.3	80	3.5	2.5
Seriously emotionally disturbed	16,400	1.1	59	2.5	3.6
Specific learning disabled	44,000	3.1	103	4.4	2.3
Speech impaired	22,200	1.6	141	6.1	6.4
Other special education	49,900	3.5	305	13.2	6.1
All other elementary	29,800	2.1	33	1.4	1.1

* In full-time equivalents.

Note: Percentages calculated on unrounded numbers. Because of rounding, details may not add to totals.

Source: Teachers in Elementary and Secondary Education, Historical Report (Washington, DC: U.S. Department of Education Center for Education Statistics), March 1987, p. 14.

Shortage per 1,000 elementary teachers by teaching field: November 1, 1983

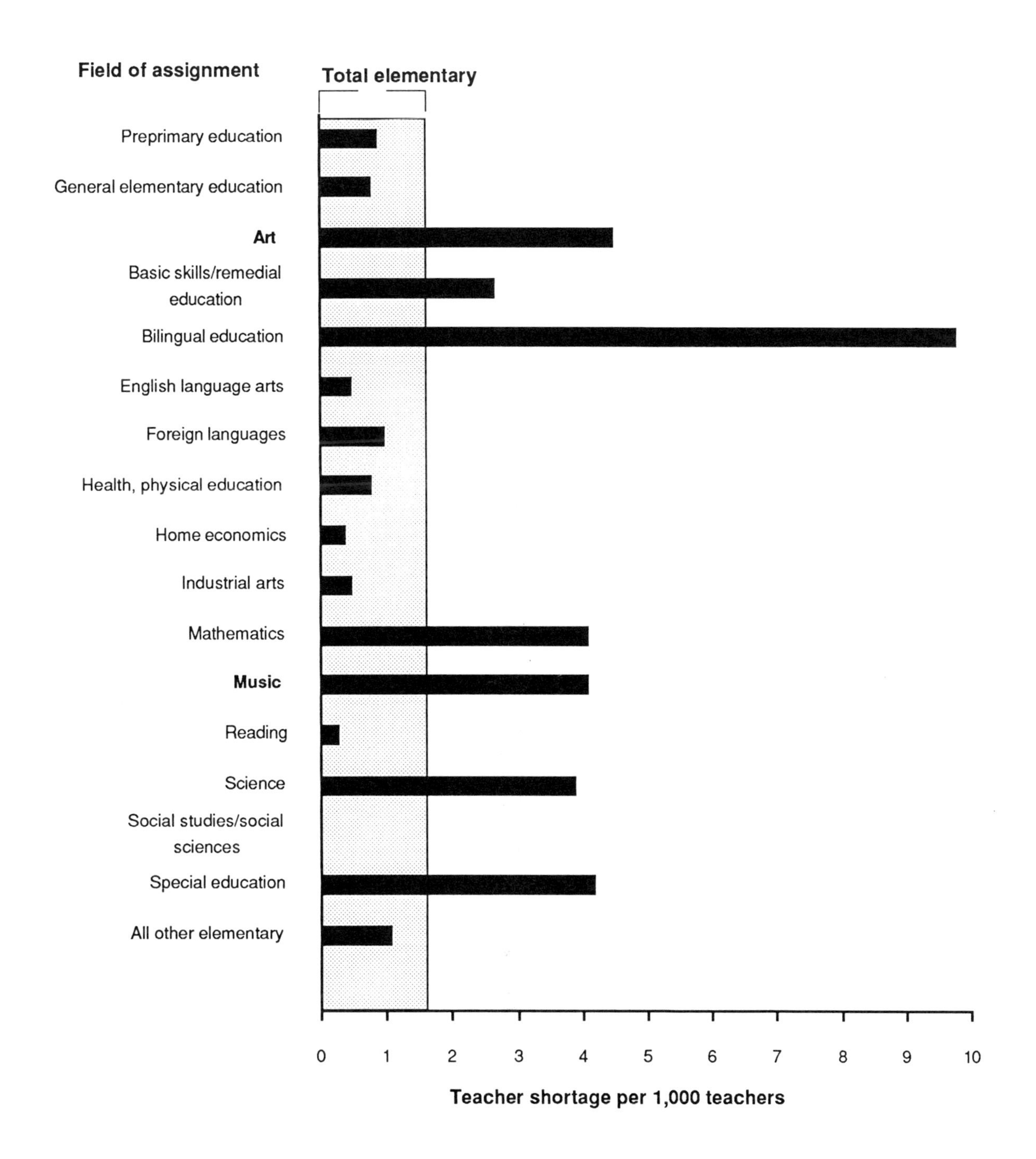

2.3 Teacher shortages: Secondary

Teacher candidate shortages* in public and private secondary schools: November 1, 1983

Field of assignment	Total teachers		Candidate shortages		Shortages per 1,000 teachers
	Number	Percentage	Number	Percentage	
Total secondary	1,124,500	100.0	1,647	100.0	1.5
Art	**31,100**	**2.8**	**95**	**5.8**	**3.1**
Basic skills/remedial education	12,300	1.1	41	2.5	3.3
Bilingual education	4,800	0.4	18	1.1	3.8
Biological and physical sciences	115,600	10.3	166	10.1	1.4
Biology	28,800	2.6	49	3.0	1.7
Chemistry	14,600	1.3	27	1.6	1.8
Physics	8,700	0.8	39	2.4	4.5
General and all other sciences	63,500	5.6	50	3.0	0.8
Business (nonvocational)	53,800	4.8	20	1.2	0.4
Computer science	9,200	0.8	34	2.1	3.7
English language arts	159,700	14.2	160	9.7	1.0
Foreign languages	46,400	4.1	73	4.4	1.6
Health, physical education	87,700	7.8	66	4.0	0.8
Home economics	34,400	3.1	26	1.6	0.8
Industrial arts	39,900	3.5	80	4.9	2.0
Mathematics	126,300	11.2	177	10.7	1.4
Music	**40,400**	**3.6**	**84**	**5.1**	**2.1**
Reading	20,500	1.8	16	1.0	0.8
Social studies/social sciences	125,600	11.2	67	4.1	0.5
Special education	99,200	8.8	337	20.5	3.4
Mentally retarded	22,000	2.0	74	4.5	3.4
Seriously emotionally disturbed	10,300	0.9	40	2.4	3.9
Specific learning disabled	29,200	2.6	87	5.3	3.0
Speech impaired	5,500	0.5	34	2.1	6.2
Other special education	32,200	2.9	103	6.3	3.2
Vocational education	64,300	5.7	68	4.1	1.1
All other secondary	53,500	4.8	119	7.2	2.2

* In full-time equivalents.

Note: Percentages calculated on unrounded numbers. Because of rounding, details may not add to totals.

Source: Teachers in Elementary and Secondary Education, Historical Report (Washington, DC: U.S. Department of Education Center for Education Statistics), March 1987, p. 15.

Shortage per 1,000 secondary teachers by teaching field: November 1, 1983

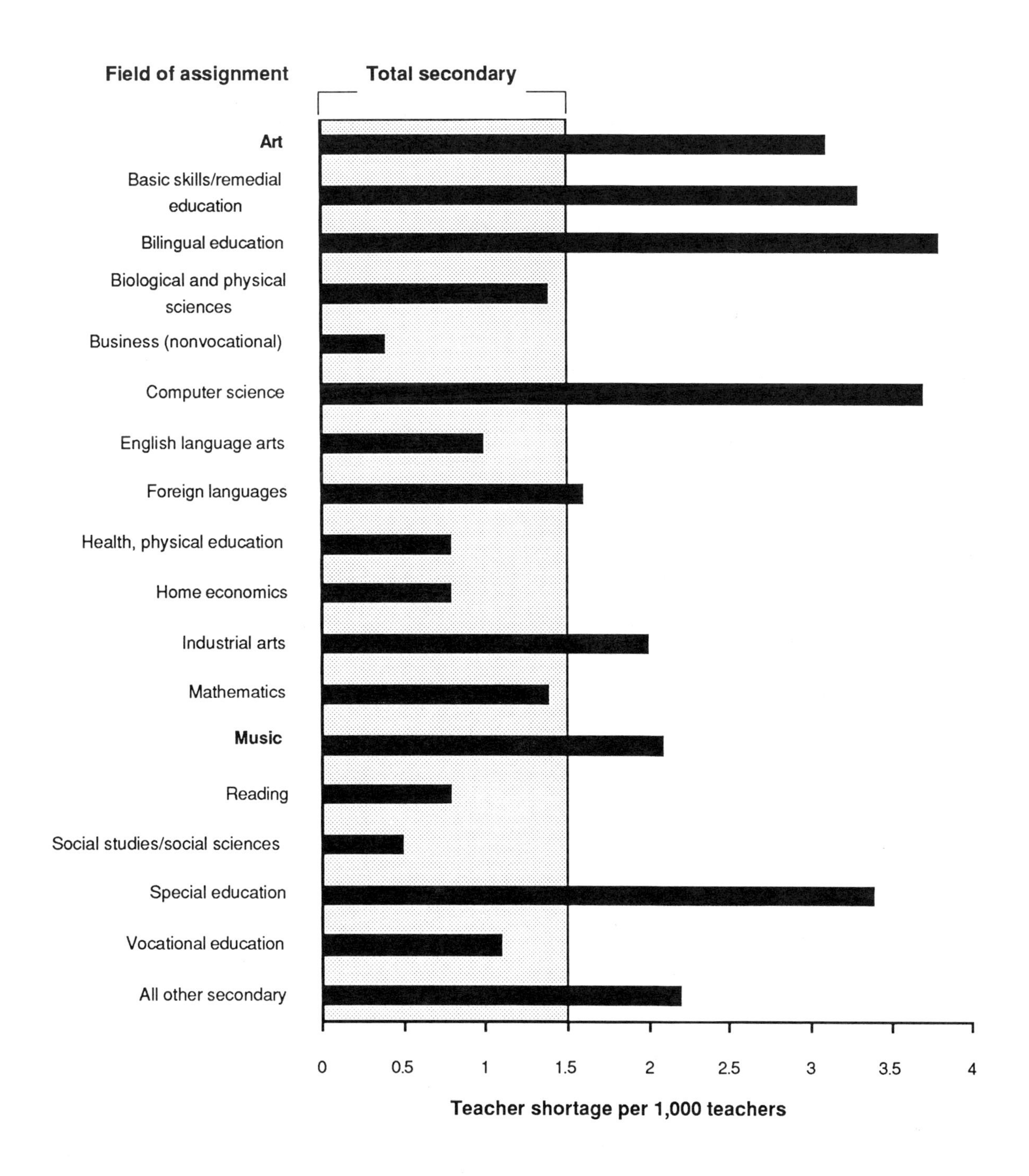

2.4 Teacher demand by region

Relative teacher supply/demand by field and geographic region: 1989

	Geographic region											
Field	AK	HI	1	2	3	4	5	6	7	8	9	Continental U.S.
Agriculture	2.00	3.00	2.67	3.00	3.50	3.08	2.14	2.83	3.33	3.00	3.00	2.93
Art	**2.00**	**1.00**	**1.40**	**2.00**	**1.56**	**2.27**	**1.80**	**2.61**	**2.52**	**2.22**	**2.67**	**2.24**
Bilingual Ed.	4.00	4.00	4.50	4.94	4.63	4.58	4.67	4.35	4.31	3.80	4.00	4.45
Business	3.00	4.00	2.91	3.18	2.29	2.68	2.61	2.96	2.63	3.28	3.25	2.84
Computer Science	4.00	—	3.38	3.67	4.00	3.80	3.67	4.00	3.74	3.45	4.00	3.75
Counselor — Elem.	4.00	4.00	3.57	2.56	3.00	3.53	3.25	3.56	3.54	3.52	3.50	3.40
Counselor — Sec.	4.00	5.00	3.38	2.83	3.14	3.55	3.05	3.04	3.52	3.45	2.73	3.26
Data Processing	—	—	3.60	3.60	3.75	3.63	3.21	3.67	3.48	3.90	4.00	3.58
Driver Ed.	—	—	2.50	2.90	3.25	2.40	2.45	2.80	3.00	2.33	3.00	2.71
Elementary — Primary	5.00	1.00	2.73	3.52	2.14	2.04	3.83	3.20	2.09	2.36	2.94	2.63
Elementary — Intermediate	5.00	1.00	2.64	3.32	2.29	2.11	3.70	3.15	2.19	2.33	2.88	2.62
English	4.00	4.00	2.64	2.96	2.00	3.10	2.91	3.37	3.02	2.81	2.67	2.97
Health Education	3.00	3.00	1.44	2.67	1.40	1.95	1.45	2.44	1.82	2.25	2.82	2.03
Home Economics	3.00	3.00	2.20	2.50	1.80	1.96	1.79	2.76	2.20	2.75	3.60	2.33
Industrial Arts	2.00	4.00	2.75	3.27	1.83	2.28	2.20	3.94	3.10	3.57	4.33	2.95
Journalism	3.00	—	2.33	2.67	1.80	3.08	2.32	2.75	2.96	3.11	3.00	2.76
Language, Mod. — French	3.00	3.00	2.55	3.05	3.14	3.50	3.50	4.09	3.61	3.55	3.33	3.51
Language, Mod. — German	3.00	3.00	2.55	2.95	3.14	3.30	3.28	3.93	3.52	3.67	3.67	3.42
Language, Mod. — Spanish	3.00	3.00	3.45	3.75	3.50	3.78	3.70	4.09	3.88	3.63	3.50	3.76
Library Science	3.00	4.00	3.60	3.40	3.50	3.71	3.55	3.63	3.63	3.60	3.75	3.60
Mathematics	5.00	4.00	3.36	4.13	3.00	3.41	4.42	4.29	3.64	3.80	4.18	3.83
Music — Instrumental	**4.00**	**1.00**	**3.50**	**3.45**	**3.22**	**3.76**	**2.77**	**2.97**	**3.00**	**2.89**	**3.00**	**3.20**
Music — Vocal	**4.00**	**1.00**	**3.50**	**2.95**	**3.25**	**3.53**	**2.50**	**2.87**	**2.73**	**2.79**	**3.11**	**3.00**
Physical Education	3.00	1.00	1.56	2.10	1.00	1.31	1.68	2.23	1.56	1.77	2.00	1.78
Psychologist (School)	5.00	—	3.80	3.50	3.83	4.22	3.42	3.68	4.11	3.53	3.38	3.79
Science — Biology	4.00	2.00	2.60	3.68	2.13	3.31	3.63	3.91	3.11	3.21	3.59	3.35
Science — Chemistry	5.00	5.00	3.18	3.83	3.38	4.04	4.13	4.34	4.02	3.85	4.31	4.01
Science — Earth	4.00	2.00	2.83	3.85	2.63	3.54	3.78	4.03	3.43	3.43	3.60	3.55
Science — General	4.00	2.00	2.83	3.67	2.50	3.49	3.50	3.97	3.28	3.28	3.50	3.43
Science — Physics	5.00	5.00	3.55	4.37	3.44	4.08	4.24	4.12	4.10	4.19	4.44	4.12
Social Sciences	3.00	5.00	1.64	2.00	1.25	1.78	1.86	2.27	1.80	2.39	2.47	1.98
Social Worker (School)	2.00	3.00	2.17	2.75	2.80	3.24	3.10	3.00	3.05	3.25	3.25	3.03
Speech	5.00	2.00	2.50	3.18	2.80	2.91	2.74	3.29	2.64	3.36	3.75	2.95
Spec. — Deaf Education	5.00	4.00	4.17	4.40	4.20	4.38	4.13	4.17	3.71	3.94	4.33	4.12
Spec. — BD	5.00	4.00	4.29	4.56	4.20	4.53	4.47	4.37	4.41	4.05	4.45	4.40
Spec. — Gifted	5.00	3.00	3.88	3.50	3.67	4.30	4.19	3.81	3.89	3.71	4.25	3.93
Spec. — LD	5.00	5.00	4.00	4.38	4.33	4.41	4.15	4.34	3.06	3.92	4.58	4.26
Spec. — Mental Handi.	5.00	5.00	4.00	4.60	4.40	4.33	4.63	4.28	4.10	4.04	4.40	4.29
Spec. — Multi. Handi.	5.00	5.00	4.38	4.58	4.40	4.33	4.53	4.25	3.25	4.14	4.30	4.14
Spec. — Reading	5.00	3.00	3.67	3.69	3.00	3.70	3.50	3.81	3.46	3.39	3.62	3.58
Speech Path./Audio.	5.00	4.00	3.57	4.33	3.86	4.29	4.33	4.30	4.48	4.05	4.25	4.25
COMPOSITE	3.88	3.11	3.04	3.43	2.94	3.27	3.32	3.57	3.21	3.30	3.52	3.32

Note: Results are based on opinion surveys of college teacher placement offices from throughout the United States. Officers were asked to use a number to indicate supply/demand, using the following: 5 = considerable shortage; 4 = some shortage; 3 = balanced; 2 = some surplus; 1 = considerable surplus. Regions are coded: Alaska; Hawaii; 1 — Northwest; 2 — West; 3 — Rocky Mountain; 4 — Great Plains/Midwest; 5 — South Central; 6 — Southeast; 7 — Great Lakes; 8 — Middle Atlantic; 9 — Northeast. Alaska and Hawaii are not included in the continental United States totals. Mailings for the 1986, 1988, and 1989 reports included all teacher placement offices that were members of ASCUS.

Source: James N. Akin, *Teacher Supply and Demand in the United States 1989 Report* (Addison, IL: Association for School, College and University Staffing, Inc.), p. 2.

Relative teacher supply/demand for art fields by geographic region: 1989

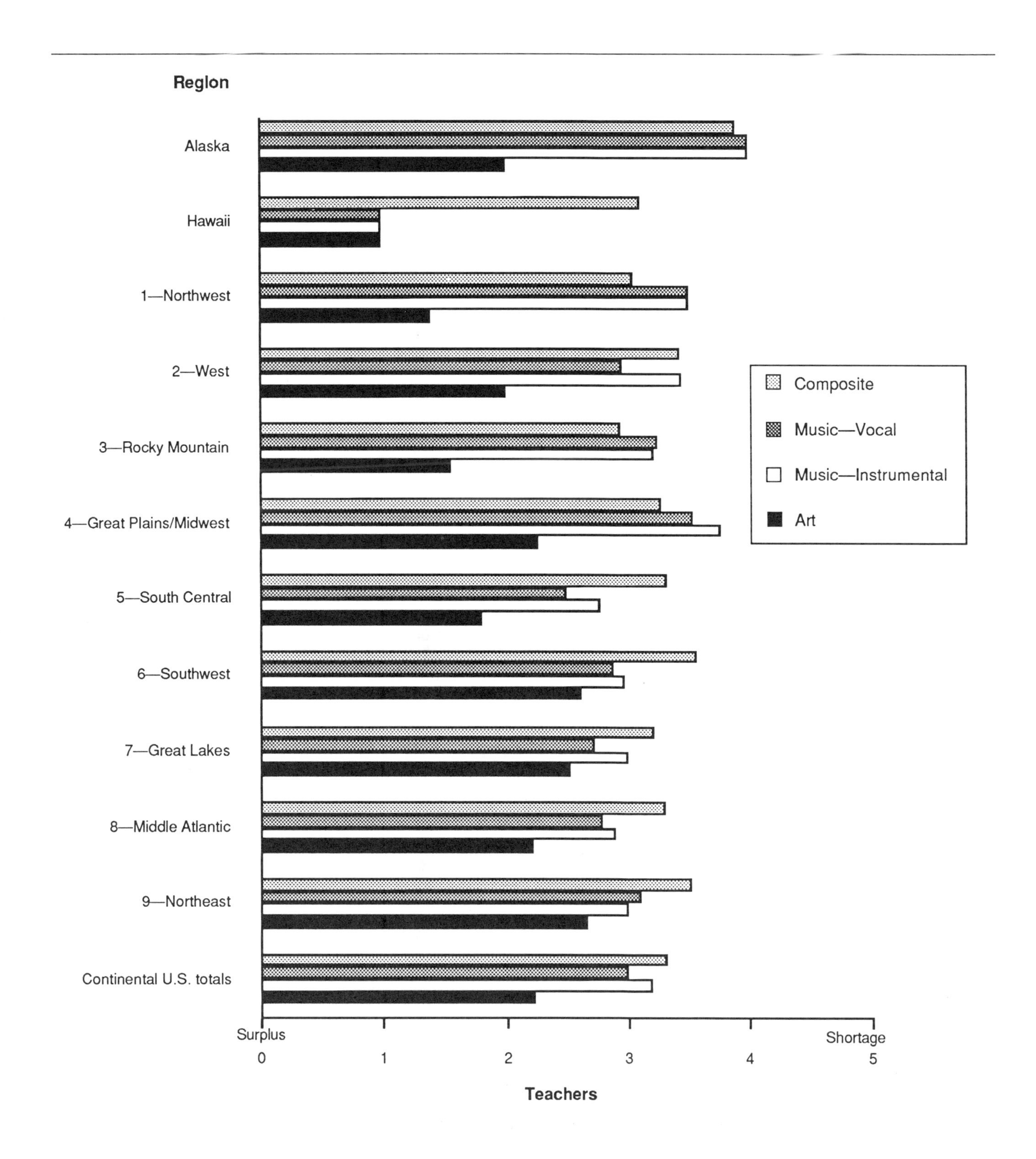

2.5 Teacher demand: 1985–1989

Relative demand by teaching area and year: 1985–1989

	1985	1986	1987	1988	1989
Teaching fields with considerable teacher shortage (5.00-4.25)					
Bilingual Education	4.12	4.27	4.42	4.35	4.45
Special Education — BD	4.02	4.20	4.30	4.33	4.40
Special Education — Ment. Handi.	3.76	4.25	3.97	4.15	4.29
Special Education — LD	3.95	4.23	4.46	4.26	4.26
Speech Pathology/Audio.	4.01	4.09	4.21	4.00	4.25
Teaching fields with some teaching shortage (4.24-3.45)					
Special Education — Multi. Handi.	3.94	4.25	3.85	4.26	4.14
Science — Physics	4.57	4.44	4.26	4.01	4.12
Special Education — Deaf	—	3.72	3.81	3.91	4.12
Science — Chemistry	4.42	4.40	4.21	3.96	4.01
Special Education — Gifted	3.85	3.91	3.88	3.74	3.93
Mathematics	4.71	4.55	4.35	4.00	3.83
Psychologist (school)	3.65	3.43	3.46	3.57	3.79
Language, Mod. — Spanish	3.43	3.64	3.57	3.59	3.76
Computer Science	4.37	4.22	3.98	3.79	3.75
Library Science	3.49	3.39	3.33	3.56	3.60
Data Processing	4.30	3.97	3.81	3.59	3.58
Special — Reading	3.39	3.46	3.45	3.43	3.58
Science — Earth	3.79	3.86	3.43	3.52	3.55
Language, Mod. — French	3.31	3.34	3.24	3.43	3.51
Teaching fields with balanced supply and demand (3.44-2.65)					
Science — General	3.65	3.82	3.32	3.42	3.43
Language, Mod. — German	3.11	3.26	3.15	3.34	3.42
Counselor — Elementary	3.05	3.04	3.31	3.12	3.40
Science — Biology	3.58	3.65	3.33	3.33	3.35
Counselor — Secondary	3.08	3.05	3.24	3.03	3.26
Music — Instrumental	**3.29**	**3.14**	**3.29**	**3.00**	**3.20**
Social Worker (school)	2.81	2.77	2.82	3.01	3.03
Music — Vocal	**3.19**	**2.95**	**3.11**	**2.89**	**3.00**
English	3.14	3.25	3.02	3.11	2.97
Industrial Arts	3.65	3.30	3.24	3.07	2.95
Speech	2.91	2.72	2.86	2.91	2.95
Agriculture	3.11	3.23	2.81	2.88	2.93
Business	3.32	3.11	2.94	2.90	2.84
Journalism	2.74	2.93	3.00	2.91	2.76
Driver Education	2.65	2.46	2.67	2.70	2.71
Teaching fields with some surplus of teachers (2.64-1.85)					
Elementary — Primary	2.57	2.70	2.58	2.71	2.63
Elementary — Intermediate	2.53	2.78	2.61	2.72	2.62
Home Economics	2.79	2.51	2.16	2.26	2.33
Art	**2.04**	**2.20**	**1.89**	**2.35**	**2.24**
Health Education	2.08	1.92	1.95	2.02	2.03
Social Science	2.17	2.11	2.05	2.00	1.98
Teaching field with considerable surplus of teachers (1.84-1.00)					
Physical Education	1.75	1.60	1.53	1.67	1.78

Note: Results are based on opinion surveys of college teacher placement offices from throughout the United States. Officers were asked to use a number to indicate supply/demand, using the following: 5 = considerable shortage; 4 = some shortage; 3 = balanced; 2 = some surplus; 1 = considerable surplus. Mailings for the 1986, 1988, and 1989 reports included all teacher placement offices that were members of ASCUS.

Source: James N. Akin, *Teacher Supply and Demand in the United States 1989 Report* (Addison, IL: Association for School, College and University Staffing, Inc.), p. 3. Used by permission of ASCUS.

Relative demand by art field and year: 1985–1989

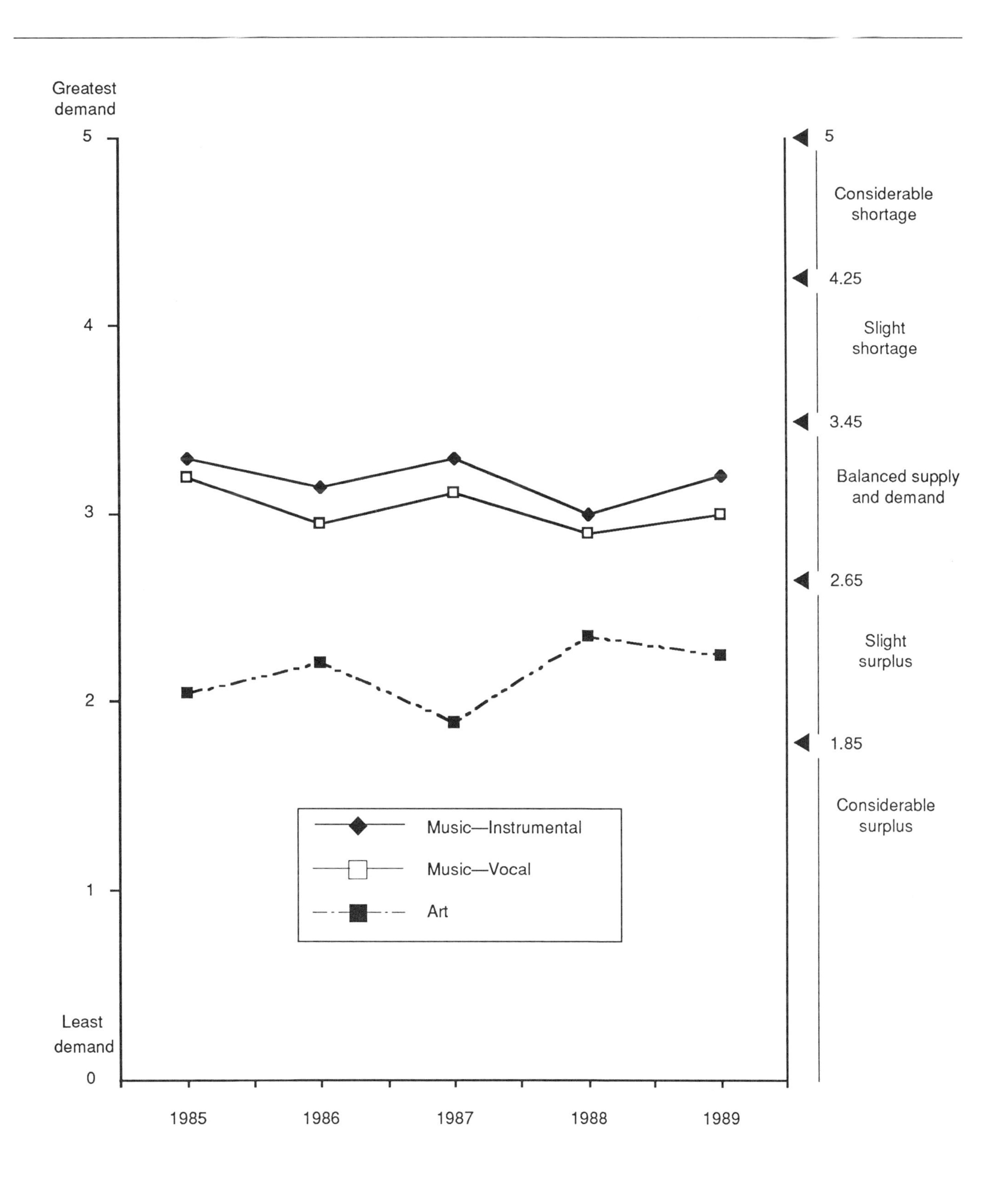

2.6 Teacher availability: Visual arts and music

Districts indicating availability of teachers in visual arts and music: 1986–1987

	Percentage of districts with surplus, balance, or shortage					
	Visual arts			Music		
District characteristic	Surplus	Balance	Shortage	Surplus	Balance	Shortage
All districts	15	64	21	16	66	18
Enrollment size						
Less than 2,500	13	64	22	15	67	18
2,500 to 9,999	19	65	16	20	67	13
10,000 or more	24	55	21	18	58	24
Metropolitan status						
Urban	18	65	17	21	64	15
Suburban	21	65	14	21	65	14
Rural	12	64	24	14	67	19
Geographic region[a]						
Northeast	14	75	11	16	70	15
Central	15	63	22	19	68	13
Southeast	18	50	32	19	62	18
West	15	65	20	11	62	27

[a] See Appendix for states in each geographic region.

Note: Percentages may not total to 100 because of rounding.

Source: Public School District Policies and Practices in Selected Aspects of Arts and Humanities Instruction (Washington, DC: U.S. Department of Education Center for Education Statistics), p. 25.

Availability of visual arts and music teachers by district characteristic: 1986–1989

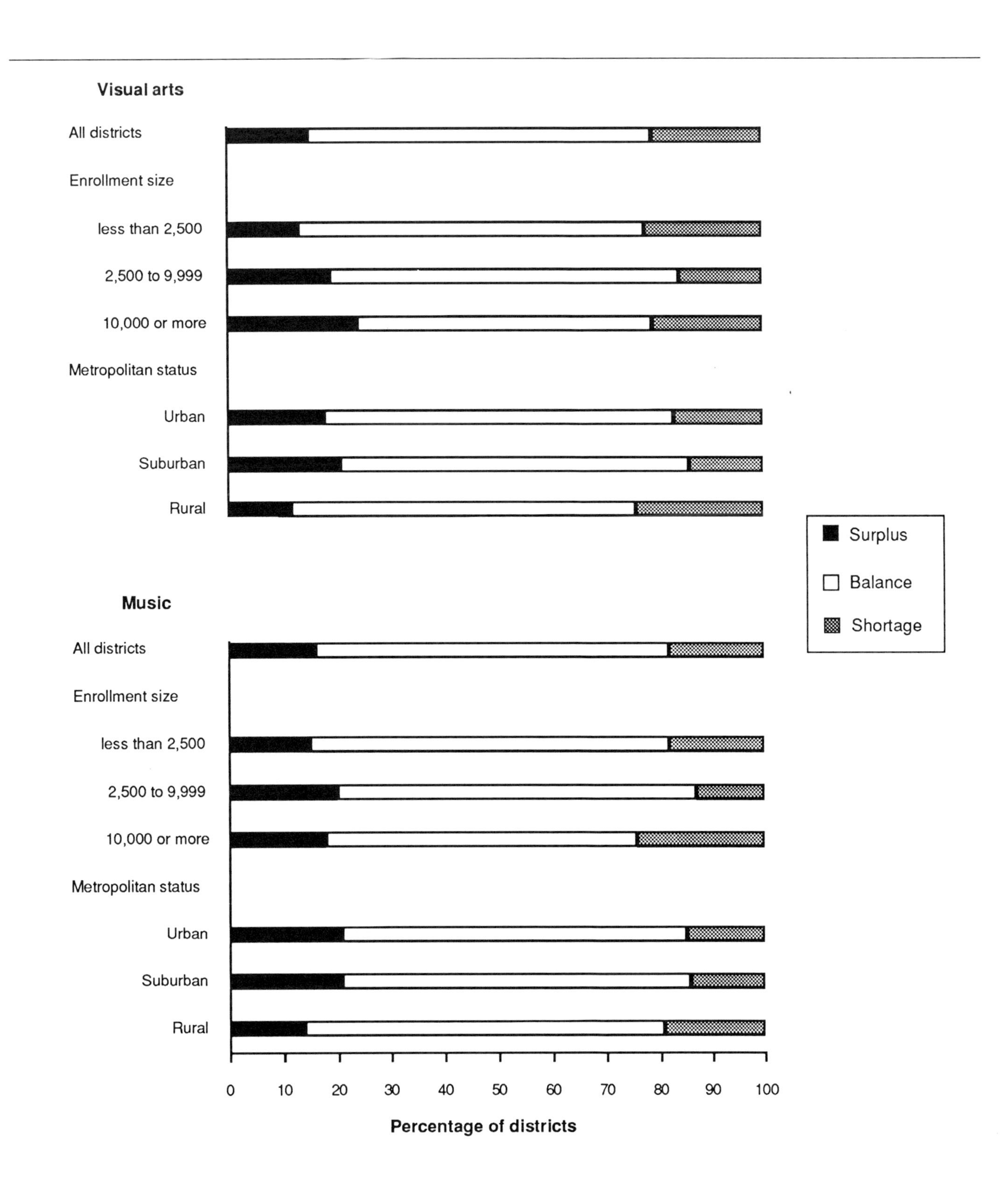

2.7 Teacher availability: Other arts

Districts indicating availability of teachers in other arts and foreign languages: 1986–1987

	Percentage of districts with surplus, balance, or shortage					
	Other arts[a]			Foreign languages		
District characteristic	**Surplus**	**Balance**	**Shortage**	**Surplus**	**Balance**	**Shortage**
All districts	10	67	23	6	54	40
Enrollment size						
Less than 2,500	8	67	24	5	54	42
2,500 to 9,999	11	71	18	9	57	34
10,000 or more	16	53	32	11	48	40
Metropolitan status						
Urban	13	60	27	9	58	34
Suburban	13	70	17	11	59	30
Rural	8	66	26	4	52	45
Geographic region[b]						
Northeast	11	72	17	9	50	41
Central	10	69	21	7	57	36
Southeast	9	62	30	4	42	54
West	8	64	28	3	59	37

[a] Dance, drama, creative writing.

[b] See Appendix for states in each geographic region.

Note: Percentages may not total to 100 because of rounding.

Source: Public School District Policies and Practices in Selected Aspects of Arts and Humanities Instruction (Washington, DC: U.S. Department of Education Center for Education Statistics), p. 26.

Availability of other arts teachers by district characteristic: 1986–1987

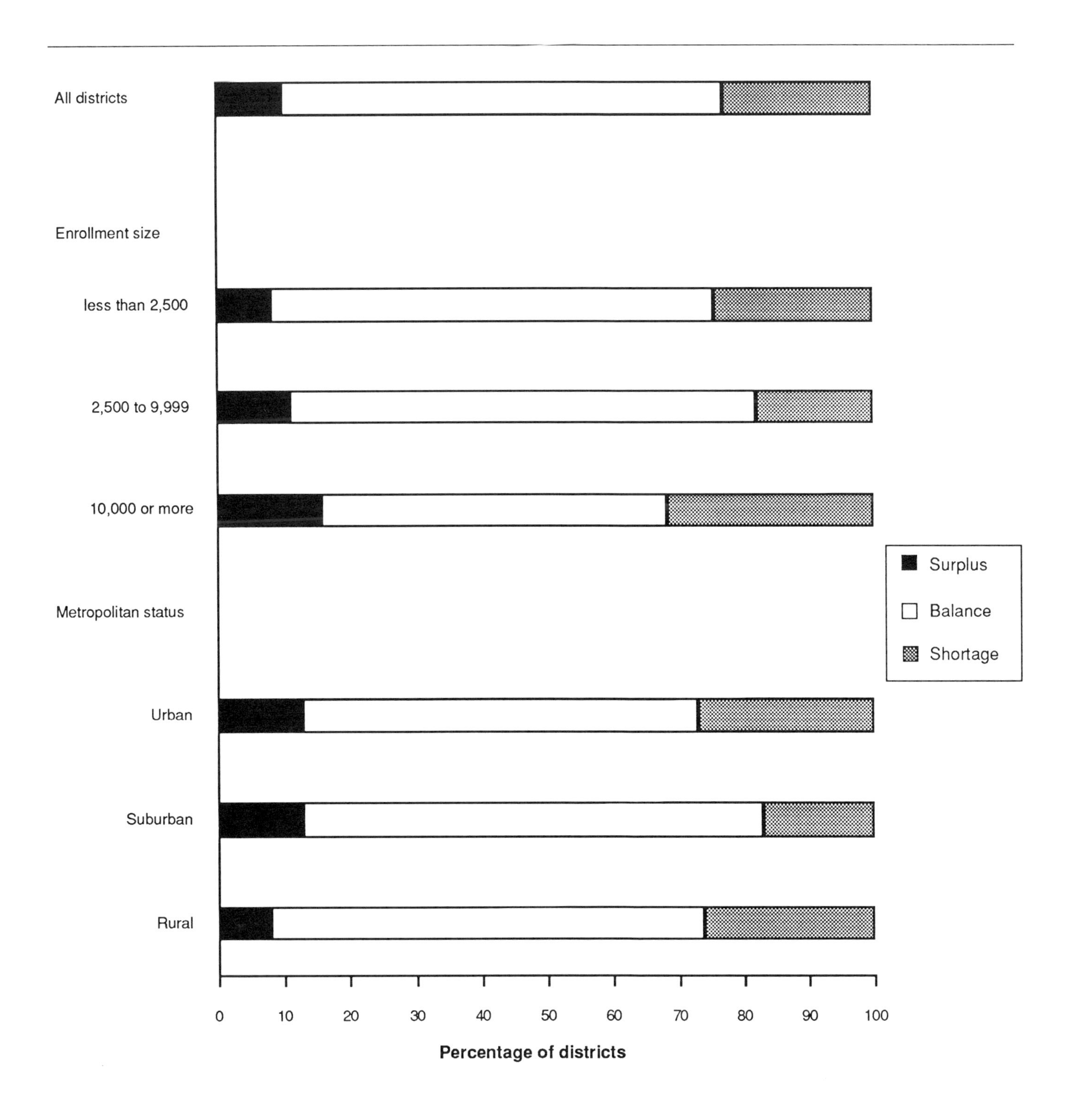

Chapter 3

Degrees

While the tables in this chapter document a dramatic decrease in the number of music education degrees awarded, these data do not necessarily predict a shortage of music teachers now or in the future. Other information, beyond the scope of this publication, is needed to determine potential shortages, e.g., current and future school enrollments and the current ages and anticipated retirement ages of those currently teaching music.

3.1 Associate degrees: 1983–1987

Associate degrees and other subbaccalaureate awards by type of curriculum: 1983–1987

Major field of study	82-83	83-84	84-85	85-86	86-87
Less than one-year subbaccalaureate awards					
All fields	29,140	33,283	36,357	38,207	43,933
Architecture and environmental design	30	32	38	34	5
Education	52	319	410	390	125
Visual and performing arts, total	1,838	1,930	1,690	1,674	1,805
Fine arts, general	0	26	24	14	4
Graphic arts technician	42	364	197	133	0
Precision production	1,773	1,432	1,278	1,313	1,680
Visual and performing arts, other	23	108	191	214	121
One-to-four-year subbaccalaureate awards					
All fields	120,024	124,633	123,680	120,380	109,613
Architecture and environmental design	293	400	411	550	593
Education	407	532	561	573	661
Visual and performing arts, total	11,048	9,811	8,926	8,380	7,962
Fine arts, general	50	57	76	69	47
Graphic arts technician	187	181	215	237	193
Precision production	10,257	8,967	8,199	7,609	7,333
Visual and performing arts, other	554	606	436	465	389
Associate degree awards					
All fields	456,441	452,416	454,712	446,047	437,137
Architecture and environmental design	1,689	1,495	1,490	1,432	1,662
Education	7,653	7,652	7,580	7,391	7,309
Visual and performing arts, total	15,284	14,503	13,742	13,961	14,560
Fine arts, general	1,422	1,074	1,033	924	1,011
Graphic arts technician	2,131	1,972	1,686	1,855	721
Precision production	8,691	9,166	8,711	9,104	9,204
Visual and performing arts, other	3,040	2,291	2,312	2,078	3,624

Note: Caution should be exercised in comparing yearly figures when the actual number of degrees conferred in a major field of study is small.

Sources: Thomas D. Snyder, *Digest of Education Statistics, 1987* (Washington, DC: U.S. Department of Education, National Center for Education Statistics), 216-17; *Digest of Education Statistics, 1988*, 191-93; *Digest of Education Statistics, 1989*, 224.

Associate-degree awards of selected curriculums as a percentage of total associate-degree awards by year: 1983–1987

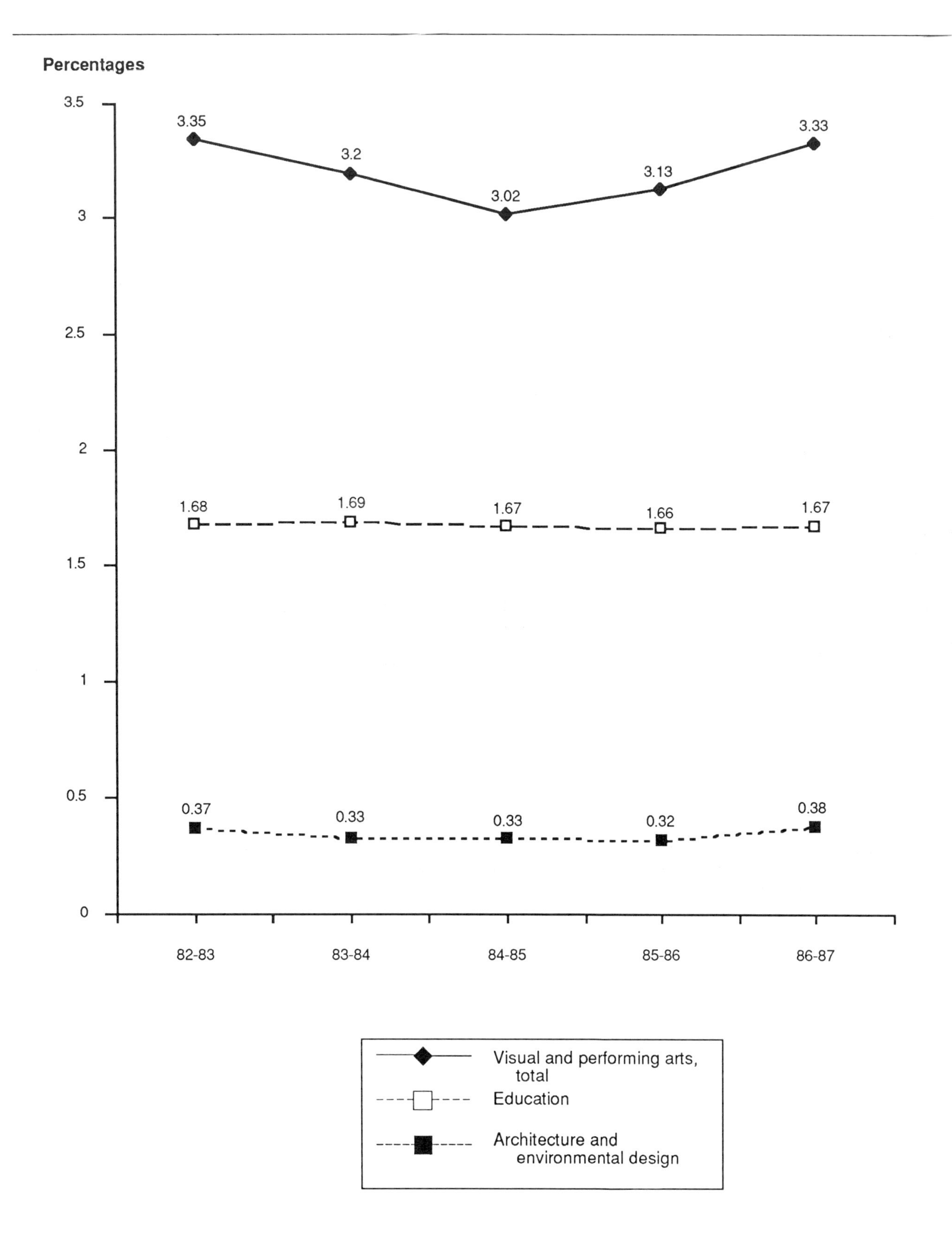

3.2 Bachelor's degrees: Recent

Bachelor's degrees requiring four or five years in selected fields, by year and by field of study: 1984–1988

Major field of study	83-84	84-85	85-86	86-87	87-88
All fields	974,309	979,477	987,823	991,339	993,362
Education (all fields)	92,382	88,161	87,221	87,115	91,013
Music education	4,085	3,671	3,330	3,109	2,904
Art education	1,428	1,272	1,070	1,213	1,021
Visual and performing arts, total[a]	39,833	37,936	36,949	36,223	36,100
Visual and performing arts, general	1,478	1,494	1,504	1,549	1,739
Crafts	417	416	364	352	392
Dance	793	730	695	675	626
Design	4,734	4,700	4,571	4,513	4,590
Dramatic arts	5,315	4,997	4,598	4,563	4,572
Film arts, total	1,647	1,551	1,648	1,639	1,737
Cinematography/film	566	515	607	615	629
Photography	787	677	682	641	648
Film arts, other	294	359	359	383	460
Fine arts, total	16,210	15,053	14,752	14,804	15,106
Fine arts, general	10,771	9,833	9,785	9,830	9,804
Art history and appreciation	1,705	1,693	1,670	1,789	1,911
Arts management	111	100	94	73	91
Painting	917	849	777	783	713
Fine arts, other	2,706	2,578	2,426	2,329	2,587
Graphic arts technology	210	180	199	0	0
Music, total	7,870	7,613	7,175	6,924	6,703
Music, general	4,323	3,919	3,730	3,697	3,242
Music history and appreciation	97	130	109	56	62
Music performance	2,532	2,615	2,481	2,313	2,372
Music theory and composition	352	297	306	276	204
Music, other	566	652	549	582	823
Precision production	272	275	298	423	—[b]
Visual and performing arts, other	887	927	1,145	781	635
Religious music	271	291	292	203	179

[a] Since data were not available for all items, there is some disparity in the totals.

[b] Data unavailable.

Note: Caution should be exercised in comparing yearly figures when the actual number of degrees conferred in a major field of study is small.

Sources: Thomas D. Snyder, *Digest of Education Statistics, 1987* (Washington, DC: U.S. Department of Education National Center for Education Statistics, 1987), 174-81; *Digest of Education Statistics, 1988*, 194-209; *Digest of Education Statistics, 1989*, 225-32; and unpublished tables by National Center for Education Statistics.

Bachelor's degrees in selected fields as a percentage of total bachelor's-degree awards by year: 1984–1988

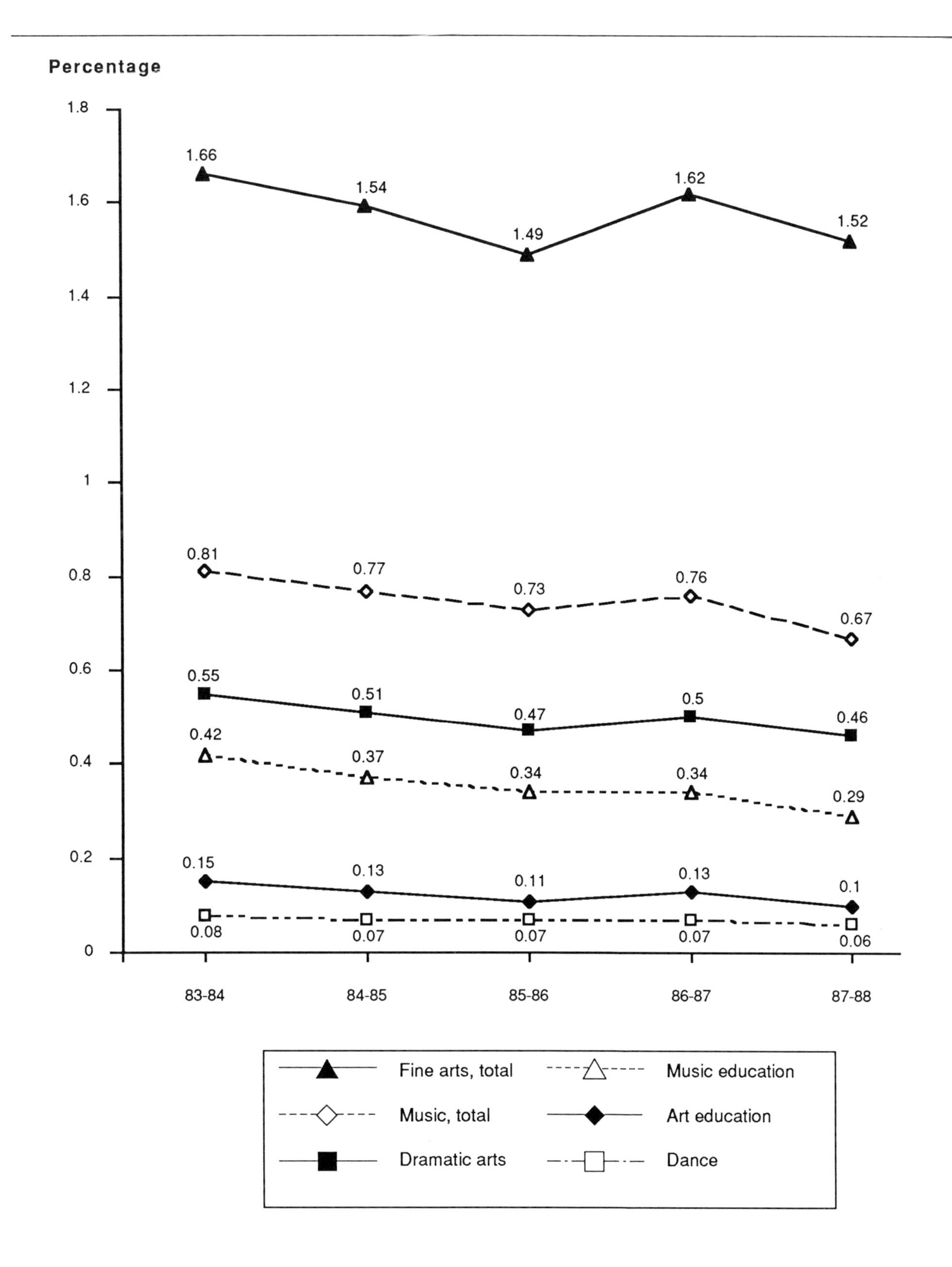

3.3 Bachelor's degrees: 1948–1988

Bachelor's degrees in selected fields, by year and field of study: 1948–1988

Major field of study	47-48[a]	52-53[a]	57-58[a]	62-63	67-68	72-73	77-78	82-83	87-88
All fields	271,348	304,857	363,502	405,427	632,289	922,362	921,204	969,510	993,362
Education (all fields)	29,635	61,420	83,283	101,752	134,905	194,210	136,079	97,991	91,013
Music education			4,753	4,955	6,457	7,483	7,376	4,378	2,904
Art education			1,645	2,573	4,457	6,215	3,637	1,695	1,021
Fine and applied arts, total	11,422[b]	16,736	12,245	14,362	25,522	36,017	40,951		
Visual and performing arts, total								39,469	36,100[c]
Visual and performing arts, general								1,652	1,739
Crafts								453	392
Dance						431	886	748	626
Applied design						1,994	3,523		
Design								4,049	4,590
Speech and dramatic arts	2,488	3,520	3,822	4,222	7,329				
Dramatic arts						4,745	5,043	5,208	4,572
Film arts, total						664[b]	1,610[b]	1,551	1,737
Cinematography/film						224	651	487	629
Photography						440	959	772	648
Film arts, other								292	460
Fine arts	3,650	—[d]							
Fine and applied arts, general			2,482	3,194	7,098	4,281	4,639		
Art						13,156	14,099		
Art history and appreciation						2,155	1,826		
Fine arts, total (for visual and performing arts)								16,107	15,106
Fine arts, general								10,847	9,804
Art history and appreciation								1,739	1,911
Arts management								206	91
Painting								846	713
Fine arts, other								2,469	2,587
Graphic arts technology								191	0
Music, total	5,284	6,546	2,872	3,031	4,169	6,749[b]	9,001[b]	7,910	6,703
Music (liberal arts program)						2,998	3,597		
Music, general								4,287	3,242
Music history and appreciation						166	169	138	62
Music (performing, composition, theory)						3,585	5,235		
Music performance								2,580	2,372
Music theory and composition								395	204
Music, other								510	823
Precision production								218	—[d]
Fine and applied arts, other		4,625	3,069	3,915	6,926	1,842	324		
Visual and performing arts, other								1,382	635
Religious music						113	294	210	179

[a] Includes first professional degrees such as M.D. and LL.B. in addition to B.S. and B.A.

[b] These totals were not given on original report.

[c] Since data were not available for all items, there is some disparity in the totals.

[d] Data unavailable.

Notes: 47-48, 52-53, 57-58, 62-63, and 67-68 figures have been recalculated from the original data to exclude the U.S. outlying areas such as Puerto Rico, Virgin Islands, and Guam. Rows within shaded areas represent essentially one category, despite differences in terminology and/or groupings of fields of study.

Sources: **47-48**, Robert C. Story, *Earned Degrees Conferred by Higher Educational Institutions 1947-48*, Circular No. 247 (Washington, DC: Federal Security Agency, Office of Education, 1948); **52-53**, Mabel C. Rice and Neva A. Carlson, *Earned Degrees Conferred by Higher Educational Institutions 1952-53* (Washington, DC: U.S. Department of Health, Education, and Welfare, Office of Education, 1953); **57-58**, Diane B. Gertler, *Earned Degrees Conferred by Higher Educational Institutions 1957-58*, Circular No. 570 (Washington, DC: U.S. Department of Health, Education, and Welfare, Office of Education, 1959); **62-63**, Patricia Wright, *Earned Degrees Conferred 1962-63, Bachelor's and Higher Degrees*, Circular No. 777, OE-54013-63 (Washington, DC: U.S. Department of Health, Education, and Welfare, Office of Education, 1965); **67-68**, Mary Evans Hooper and Marjorie O. Chandler, *Earned Degrees Conferred: Part A—Summary Data* and *Earned Degrees Conferred: Part B—Institutional Data* (Washington, DC: U.S. Department of Health, Education, and Welfare, Office of Education, 1969); **72-73**, W. Vance Grant and George C. Lind, *Digest of Education Statistics, 1975* (Washington, DC: National Center for Education Statistics, U.S. Department of Health, Education, and Welfare, 1976), 108-13; **77-78**, W. Vance Grant and Leo J. Eiden, *Digest of Education Statistics, 1980* (Washington, DC: National Center for Education Statistics, 1980), 120-24; **82-83**, Thomas D. Snyder, *Digest of Education Statistics, 1987* (Washington, DC: Center for Education Statistics, 1987), 182-89; **87-88**, unpublished tables by National Center for Education Statistics.

3.3a Bachelor's degrees: 1948–1988

Bachelor's degrees in selected fields, as a percentage of total bachelor's-degree awards by year: 1948–1988

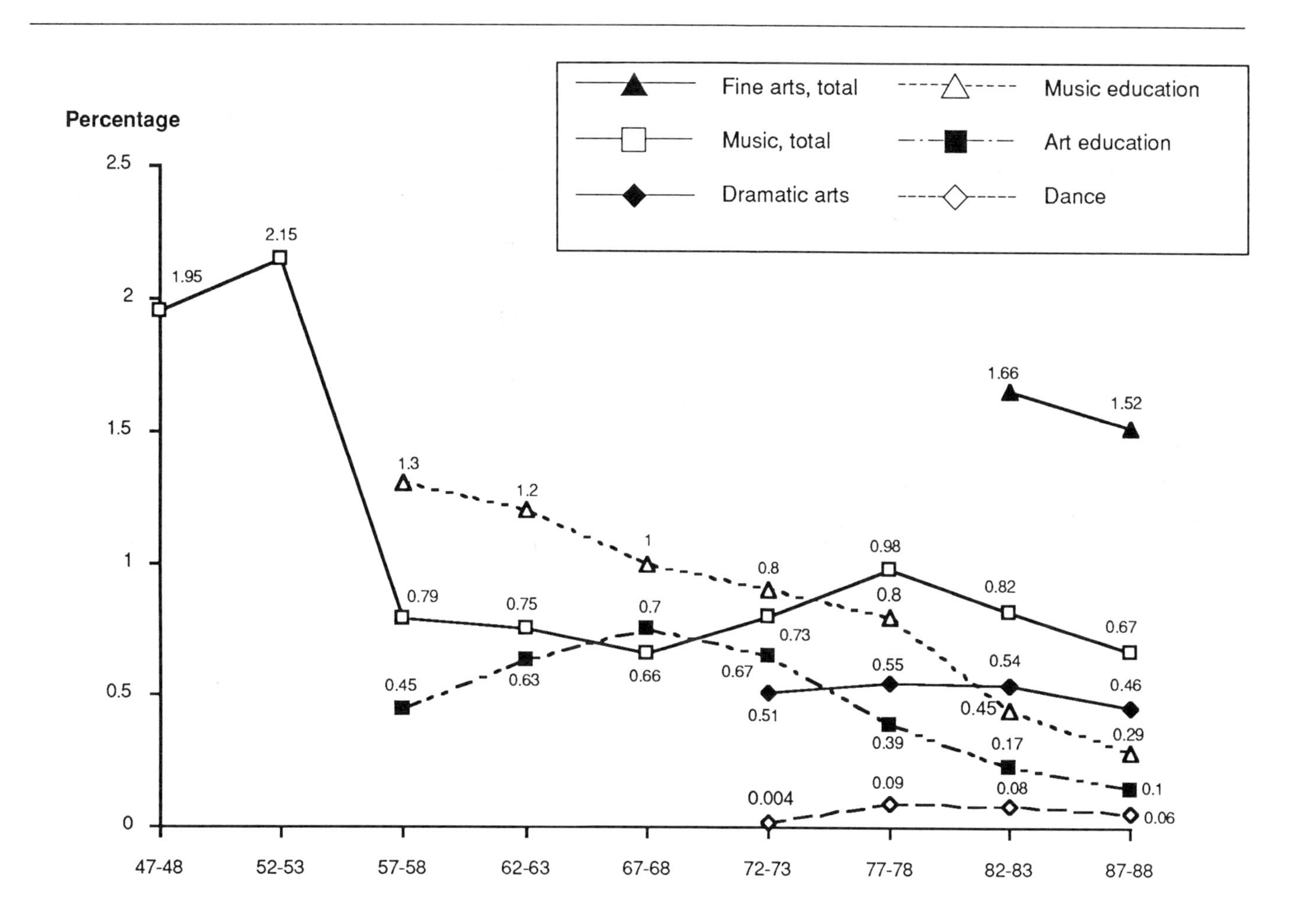

3.4 Master's degrees: Recent

Master's degrees in selected fields, by year and by field of study: 1983–1988

Major field of study	83-84	84-85	85-86	86-87	87-88
All fields	284,263	286,251	288,567	289,557	298,733
Education (all fields)	77,187	76,137	76,353	75,501	77,704
Music education	920	945	862	955	858
Art education	589	579	511	620	443
Visual and performing arts, total[a]	8,520	8,714	8,416	8,506	7,920
Visual and performing arts, general	192	220	177	227	191
Crafts	60	56	60	88	96
Dance	174	236	197	186	174
Design	254	267	291	279	289
Dramatic arts	1,181	1,175	1,192	1,108	1,068
Film arts, total	309	316	219	368	226
Cinematography/film	192	203	118	213	130
Photography	84	84	73	86	70
Film arts, other	33	29	28	69	26
Fine arts, total	2,819	2,824	2,727	2,738	2,612
Fine arts, general	1,634	1,564	1,536	1,573	1,479
Art history and appreciation	389	401	362	386	386
Arts management	42	67	83	69	70
Painting	181	200	169	177	173
Fine arts, other	573	592	577	533	504
Graphic arts technology	9	16	19	0	0
Music, total	3,450	3,533	3,453	3,454	3,192
Music, general	1,360	1,418	1,302	1,249	1,023
Music history and appreciation	69	59	64	52	55
Music performance	1,583	1,651	1,656	1,629	1,642
Music theory and composition	222	160	189	218	127
Music, other	216	245	242	306	345
Precision production	0	4	1	3	—[b]
Visual and performing arts, other	72	67	80	55	72
Religious music	106	148	130	126	100

[a] Since data were not available for all items, there is some disparity in the totals.

[b] Data unavailable.

Note: Caution should be exercised in comparing yearly figures when the actual number of degrees conferred in a major field of study is small.

Sources: Thomas D. Snyder, *Digest of Education Statistics, 1987* (Washington, DC: U.S. Department of Education, National Center for Education Statistics), 174-81; *Digest of Education Statistics, 1988*, 194-209; *Digest of Education Statistics, 1989*, 225-32; and unpublished tables by National Center for Education Statistics.

Master's degrees in selected fields as a percentage of total master's-degree awards by year: 1983–1988

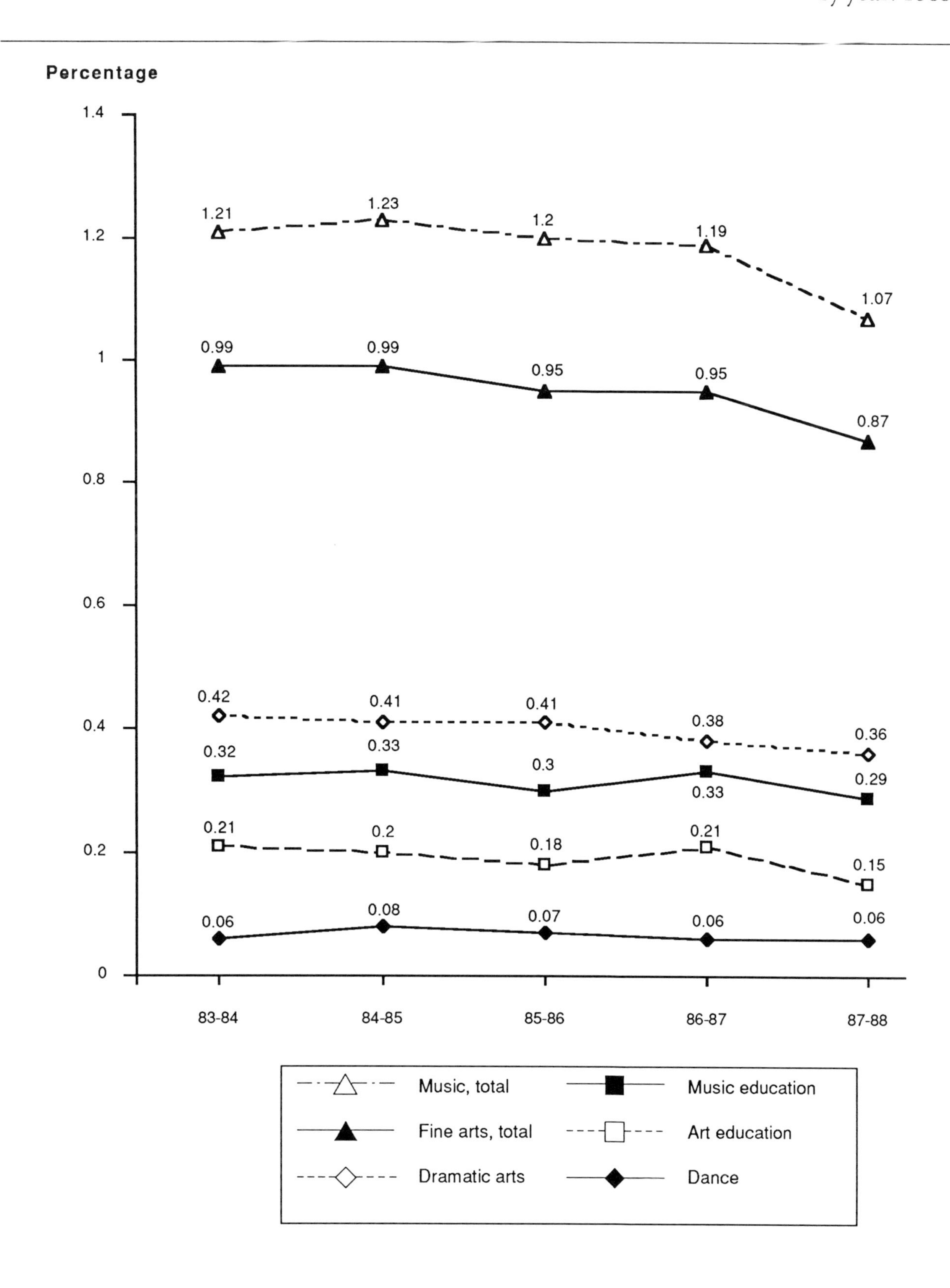

3.5 Master's degrees: 1948–1988

Master's degrees in selected fields, by year and field of study: 1948–1988

Major field of study	47-48	52-53	57-58	62-63	67-68	72-73	77-78	82-83	87-88
All fields	42,412	61,003	65,586	90,993	176,749	263,371	311,620	289,921	298,733
Education (all fields)	11,934	26,827	31,112	37,512	63,506	105,242	118,582	84,853	77,704
Music education			1,028	1,230	1,582	1,483	1,355	1,017	858
Art education			142	450	832	1,103	966	640	443
Fine and applied arts, total	2,063[a]	3,379	2,448	3,352	6,563	7,254	9,036		
Visual and performing arts, total								8,742	7,920[b]
Visual and performing arts, general								200	191
Crafts								85	96
Dance						104	205	202	174
Applied design						173	282		
Design								248	289
Speech and dramatic arts	541	880	761	1,043	2,071				
Dramatic arts						979	1,295	1,157	1,068
Film arts, total						129[a]	236[a]	293	226
Cinematography/film						82	147	156	130
Photography						47	89	89	70
Film arts, other								48	26
Fine arts	479	—[c]							
Fine arts and applied arts, general			346	488	1,341	686	668		
Art						1,793	2,333		
Art history and appreciation						383	406		
Fine arts, total (for visual and performing arts)								2,833	2,612
Fine arts, general								1,596	1,479
Art history and appreciation								382	386
Arts management								55	70
Painting								202	173
Fine arts, other								598	504
Graphic arts technology								16	0
Music, total	1,043	1,694	1,010	1,191	1,898	2,652[a]	3,464[a]	3,551	3,192
Music (liberal arts program)						692	698		
Music, general								1,437	1,023
Music history and appreciation						94	98	148	55
Music (performance, composition, theory)						1,866	2,668		
Music performance								1,554	1,642
Music theory and composition								231	127
Music, other								181	345
Precision production								0	—[c]
Fine and applied arts, other		612	331	630	1,253	355	147		
Visual and performing arts, other								157	72
Religious music						120	142	133	100

[a] These totals were not given on original report.

[b] Since data were not available for all items, there is some disparity in the totals.

[c] Data unavailable.

Notes: 47-48, 52-53, 57-58, 62-63, and 67-68 figures have been recalculated from the original data to exclude the U.S. outlying areas such as Puerto Rico, Virgin Islands, and Guam. Rows within shaded areas represent essentially one category, despite differences in terminology and/or groupings of fields of study.

Sources: **47-48**, Robert C. Story, *Earned Degrees Conferred by Higher Educational Institutions 1947-48*, Circular No. 247 (Washington, DC: Federal Security Agency, Office of Education, 1948); **52-53**, Mabel C. Rice and Neva A. Carlson, *Earned Degrees Conferred by Higher Educational Institutions 1952-53* (Washington, DC: U.S. Department of Health, Education, and Welfare, Office of Education, 1953); **57-58**, Diane B. Gertler, *Earned Degrees Conferred by Higher Educational Institutions 1957-58*, Circular No. 570 (Washington, DC: U.S. Department of Health, Education, and Welfare, Office of Education, 1959); **62-63**, Patricia Wright, *Earned Degrees Conferred 1962-63, Bachelor's and Higher Degrees*, Circular No. 777, OE-54013-63 (Washington, DC: U.S. Department of Health, Education, and Welfare, Office of Education, 1965); **67-68**, Mary Evans Hooper and Marjorie O. Chandler, *Earned Degrees Conferred: Part A—Summary Data* and *Earned Degrees Conferred: Part B—Institutional Data* (Washington, DC: U.S. Department of Health, Education, and Welfare, Office of Education, 1969); **72-73**, W. Vance Grant and George C. Lind, *Digest of Education Statistics, 1975* (Washington, DC: National Center for Education Statistics, U.S. Department of Health, Education, and Welfare, 1976), 108-13; **77-78** W. Vance Grant and Leo J. Eiden, *Digest of Education Statistics, 1980* (Washington, DC: National Center for Education Statistics, 1980), 120-24; **82-83**, Thomas D. Snyder, *Digest of Education Statistics, 1987* (Washington, DC: Center for Education Statistics, 1987), 182-89; **87-88**, unpublished tables by National Center for Education Statistics.

3.5a Master's degrees: 1948–1988

Master's degrees in selected fields as a percentage of total master's-degree awards by year: 1948–1988

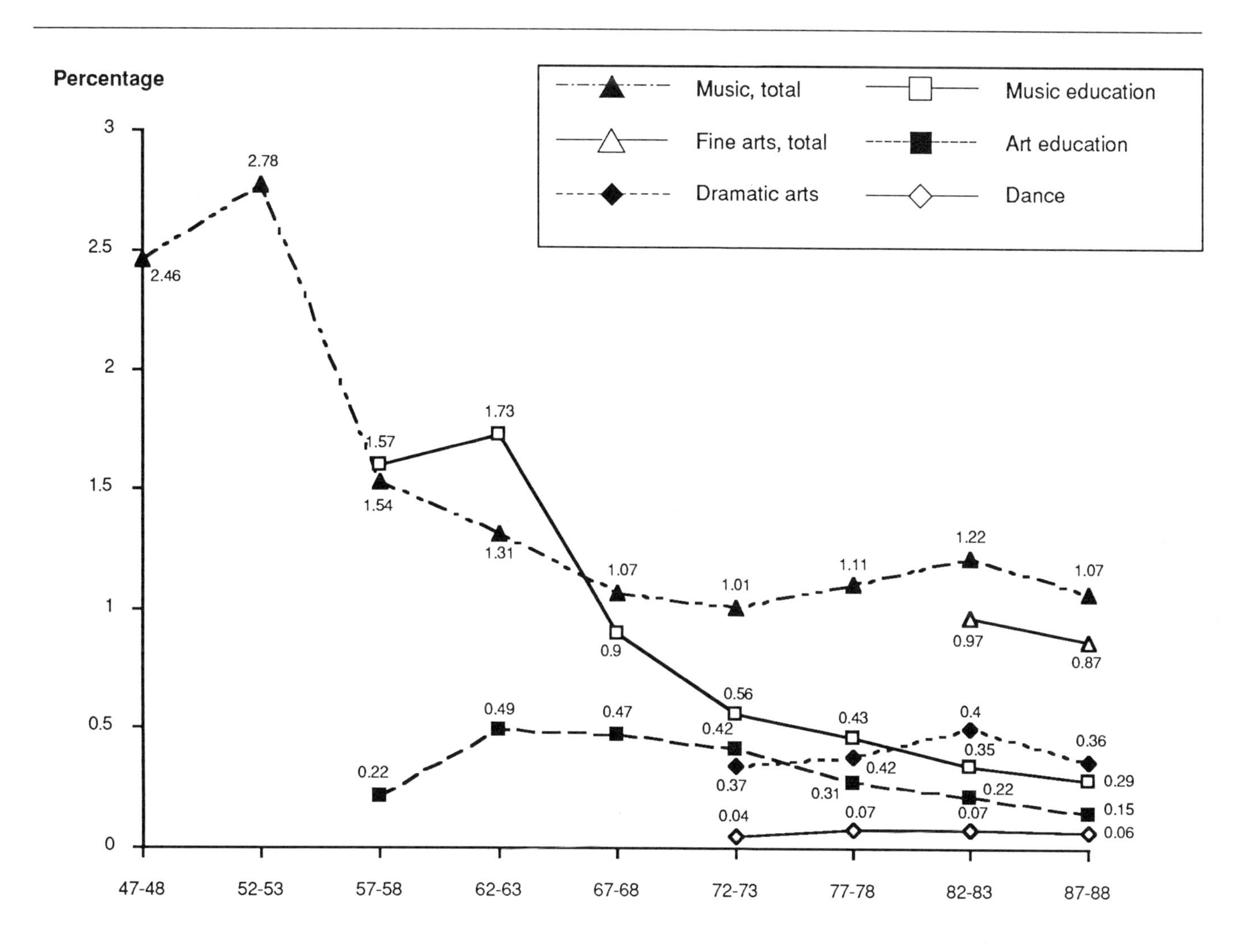

Doctoral degrees in selected fields, by year and by field of study: 1984–1988

Major field of study	83-84	84-85	85-86	86-87	87-88
All fields	33,209	32,943	33,653	34,120	34,839
Education (all fields)	7,473	7,151	7,110	6,909	6,544
Music education	73	75	80	87	64
Art education	42	23	39	49	33
Visual and performing arts, total[a]	728	693	722	792	728
Visual and performing arts, general	10	4	5	1	3
Crafts	0	0	0	0	0
Dance	3	6	5	4	6
Design	0	0	0	0	0
Dramatic arts	100	83	74	84	76
Film arts, total	5	5	6	6	1
Cinematography/film	5	4	4	6	1
Photography	0	1	0	0	0
Film arts, other	0	0	2	0	0
Fine arts, total	147	161	154	175	139
Fine arts, general	23	35	34	44	28
Art history and appreciation	106	105	95	110	97
Arts management	1	1	1	1	1
Painting	0	1	0	0	0
Fine arts, other	17	19	24	20	13
Graphic arts technology	5	0	0	0	0
Music, total	458	432	476	518	502
Music, general	216	205	231	236	209
Music history and appreciation	32	19	27	29	33
Music performance	116	133	156	164	166
Music theory and composition	84	51	44	53	54
Music, other	10	24	18	36	40
Precision production	0	0	0	0	—[b]
Visual and performing arts, other	0	2	2	4	1
Religious music	6	8	6	6	5

[a] Since data were not available for all items, there is some disparity in the totals.

[b] Data unavailable.

Note: Caution should be exercised in comparing yearly figures when the actual number of degrees conferred in a major field of study is small.

Sources: Thomas D. Snyder, *Digest of Education Statistics, 1987* (Washington, DC: U.S. Department of Education National Center for Education Statistics), 174-81; *Digest of Education Statistics, 1988*, 194-209; *Digest of Education Statistics, 1989*, 225-32; and unpublished tables by National Center for Education Statistics.

Doctoral degrees in selected fields, as a percentage of total doctoral-degree awards by year: 1983–1988

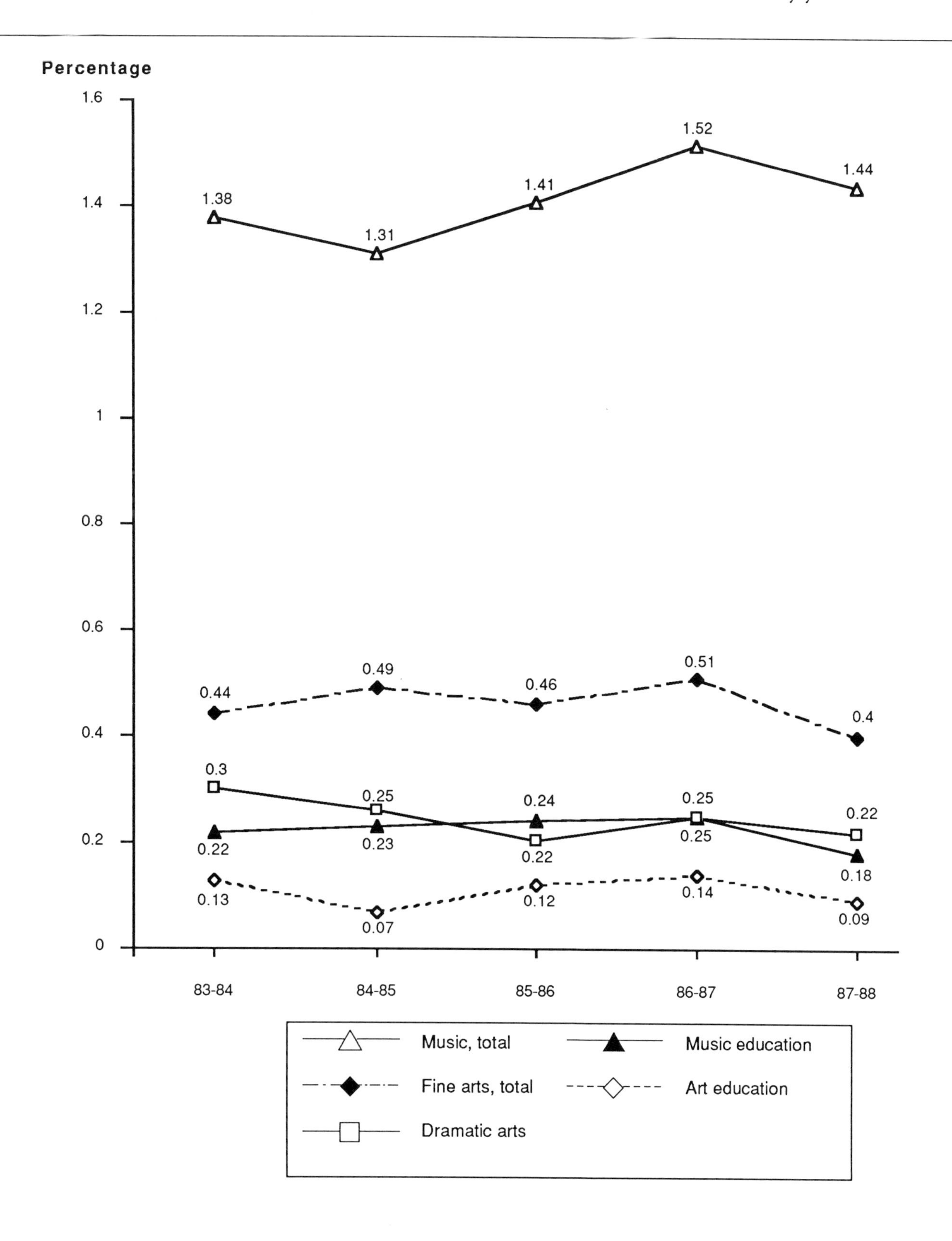

3.7 Doctoral degrees—1948–1988

Doctoral degrees in selected fields, by year and by field of study: 1948–1988

Major field of study	47-48	52-53	57-58	62-63	67-68	72-73	77-78	82-83	87-88
All fields	4,188	8,309	8,942	12,820	23,089	34,777	32,131	32,775	34,839
Education (all fields)	502	1,357	1,638	2,075	4,079	7,314	7,586	7,551	6,544
Music education			41	46	81	95	66	65	64
Art education			5	20	35	36	40	47	33
Fine and applied arts, total	92[b]	207	219	377	528	616	708		
Visual and performing arts, total								692	728[b]
Visual and performing arts, general								10	3
Crafts								0	0
Dance						1	0	4	6
Applied design						0	1		
Design								1	0
Speech and dramatic arts	52	121	102	185	269				
Dramatic arts						92	116	97	76
Film arts, total						0[a]	3[a]	6	1
Cinematography/film						0	2	6	1
Photography						0	1	0	0
Film arts, other								0	0
Fine arts	13	—[c]							
Fine and applied arts, general			10	1	24	53	76		
Art						12	6		
Art history and appreciation						67	109		
Fine arts, total (for visual and performing arts)								153	139
Fine arts, general								22	28
Art history and appreciation								112	97
Arts management								2	1
Painting								0	0
Fine arts, other								17	13
Graphic arts technology								0	0
Music, total	27	61	74	154	185	366[a]	395[a]	421	502
Music (liberal arts program)						68	88		
Music, general								214	209
Music history and appreciation						53	41	26	33
Music (performing, composition, theory)						245	266		
Music performance								103	166
Music theory and composition								63	54
Music, other								15	40
Precision production								0	—[c]
Fine and applied arts, other		21	33	37	50	25	2		
Visual and performing arts, other								0	1
Religious music						7	5	19	5

[a] These totals were not given on original report.

[b] Since data were not available for all items, there is some disparity in the totals.

[c] Data unavailable.

Notes: 47-48, 52-53, 57-58, 62-63, and 67-68 figures have been recalculated from the original data to exclude the U.S. outlying areas such as Puerto Rico, Virgin Islands, and Guam. Rows within shaded areas represent essentially one category, despite differences in terminology and/or groupings of fields of study.

Sources: **47-48**, Robert C. Story, *Earned Degrees Conferred by Higher Educational Institutions 1947-48*, Circular No. 247 (Washington, DC: Federal Security Agency, Office of Education, 1948); **52-53**, Mabel C. Rice and Neva A. Carlson, *Earned Degrees Conferred by Higher Educational Institutions 1952-53* (Washington, DC: U.S. Department of Health, Education, and Welfare, Office of Education, 1953); **57-58**, Diane B. Gertler, *Earned Degrees*

Conferred by Higher Educational Institutions 1957-58, Circular No. 570 (Washington, DC: U.S. Department of Health, Education, and Welfare, Office of Education, 1959); **62-63**, Patricia Wright, *Earned Degrees Conferred 1962-63, Bachelor's and Higher Degrees*, Circular No. 777, OE-54013-63 (Washington, DC: U.S. Department of Health, Education, and Welfare, Office of Education, 1965); **67-68**, Mary Evans Hooper and Marjorie O. Chandler, *Earned Degrees Conferred: Part A—Summary Data* and *Earned Degrees Conferred: Part B—Institutional Data* (Washington, DC: U.S. Department of Health, Education, and Welfare, Office of Education, 1969); **72-73**, W. Vance Grant and George C. Lind, *Digest of Education Statistics, 1975* (Washington, DC: National Center for Education Statistics, U.S. Department of Health, Education, and Welfare, 1976), 108-13; **77-78** W. Vance Grant and Leo J. Eiden, *Digest of Education Statistics, 1980* (Washington, DC: National Center for Education Statistics, 1980), 120-24; **82-83**, Thomas D. Snyder, *Digest of Education Statistics, 1987* (Washington, DC: Center for Education Statistics, 1987), 182-89; **87-88**, unpublished tables by National Center for Education Statistics.

3.7a Doctoral degrees: 1948–1988

Doctoral degrees in selected fields as a percentage of total doctoral-degree awards by year: 1948–1988

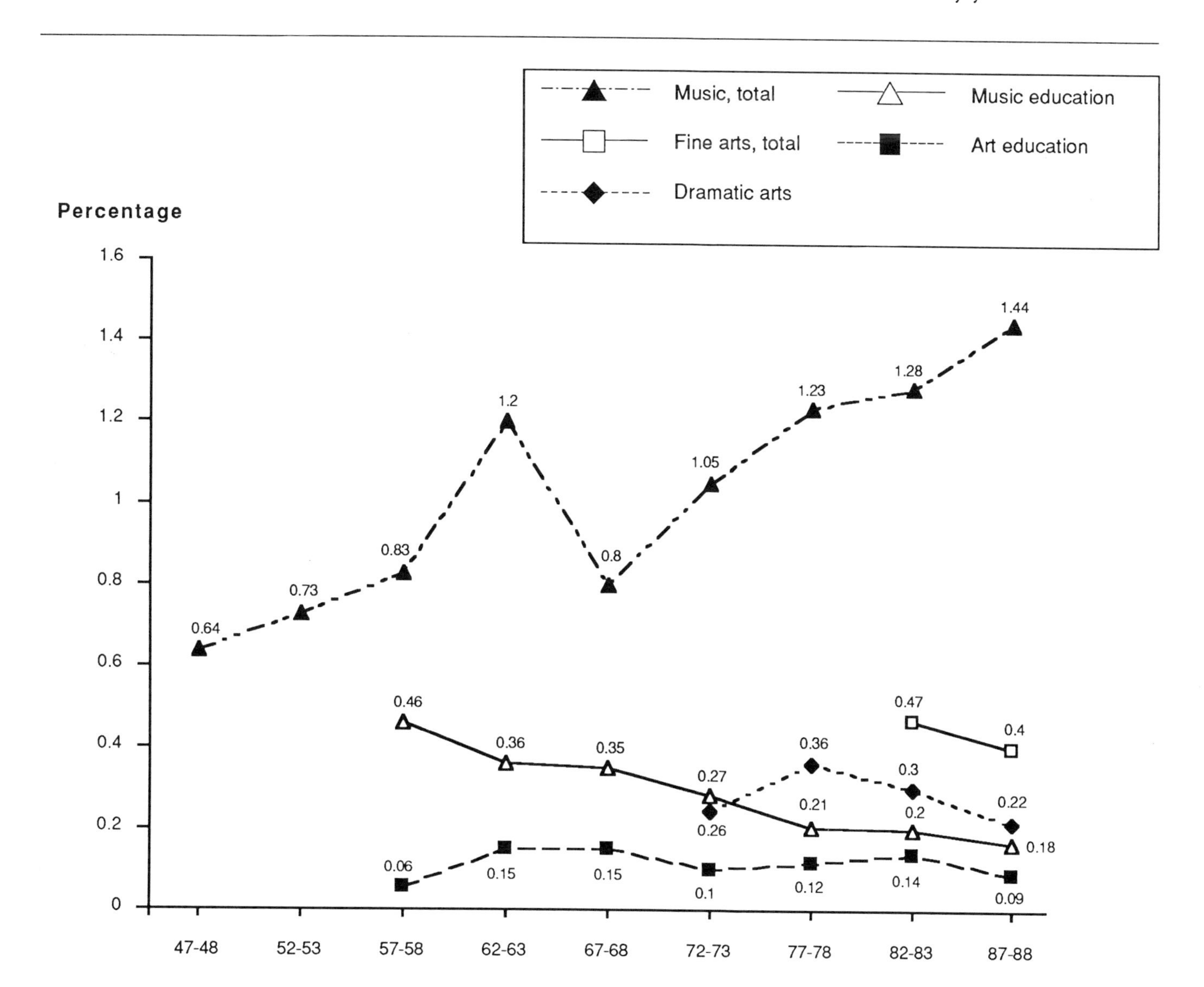

3.8 Graduate-level arts programs

Arts-related graduate and professional programs: 1990

Study area	Graduate-level programs	Master's programs	Ph.D. programs
Applied arts and design	134	69	7
Architecture	82	81	18
Art education	150	149	17
Art/fine arts	239	237	30
Art history	117	112	44
Art therapy	28	27	2
Arts administration	23	21	3
Dance	47	47	8
Dance, drama, and music therapy	20	19	1
Drama/theatre arts	175	172	39
Folklore	8	7	4
Graphic design	59	58	1
Illustration	18	18	—
Industrial design	22	22	1
Interior design	45	45	2
Landscape architecture	35	35	5
Museum studies	28	24	1
Music	309	306	87
Music education	192	190	36
Photography	59	58	1
Radio, television, and film	94	94	19
Textile design	39	39	3
Urban design	16	15	1
Writing	101	99	13

Note: — = none listed. Arts-related programs are among the areas of study listed in the guide.

Source: vonVorys, Beverly, Series Editor, Horrower III, Gordon, and Jacobs, James E., Data Editors, *Graduate and Professional Programs: An Overview, 1990,* 24th edition, *Peterson's Annual Guides to Graduate Study: Book 1,* Princeton, NJ, 1989, pp. 30–115.

3.8a Graduate-level arts programs

Arts-related master's and Ph.D. programs: 1990

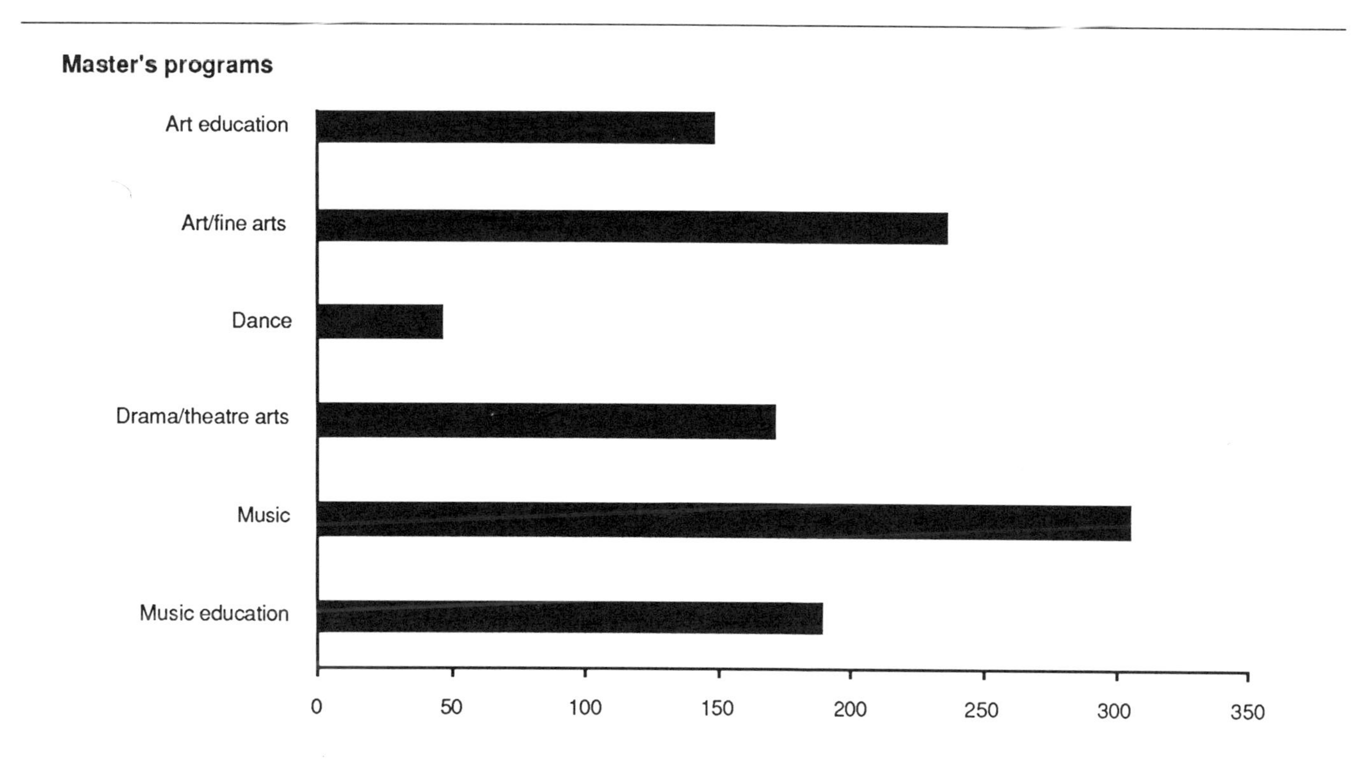

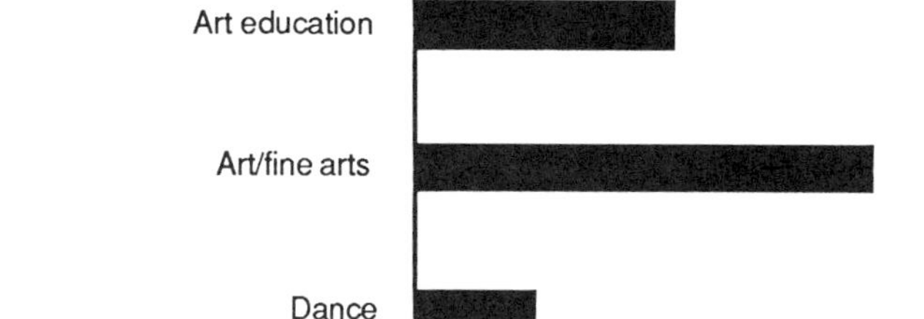

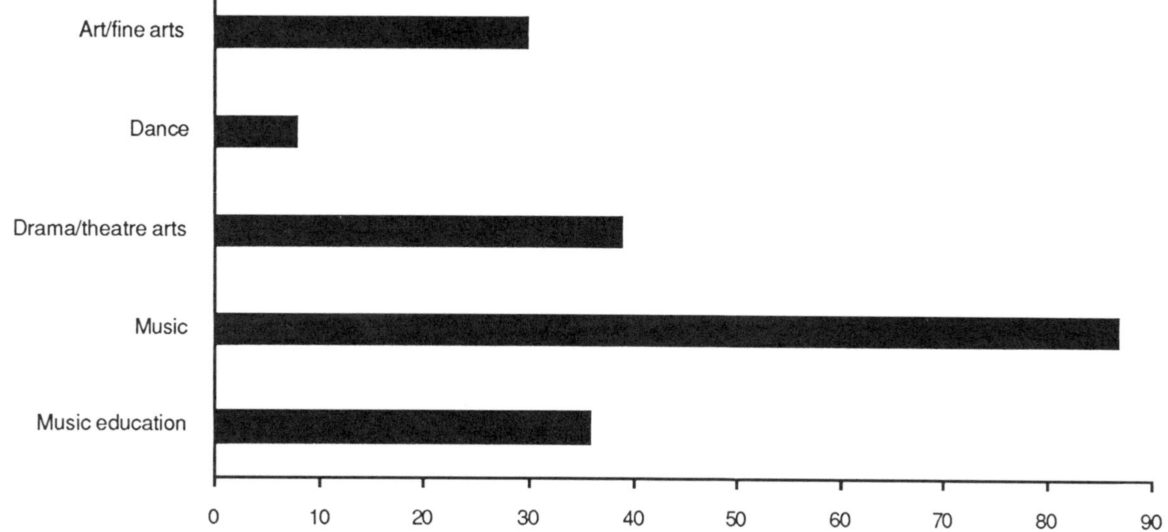

Chapter 4

Examinations

Though the National Assessment of Educational Progress reports in this chapter present data from the 1970s, these data are the most recent nationally based data on elementary/secondary student achievement in art and music.

Recent changes in personal questions asked of Scholastic Aptitude Test (SAT) takers provide data that show that the mean scores for students who take arts courses are higher than the mean scores for those who do not take course work in the arts. In addition, the mean scores for arts-course takers also surpass the scores for the population as a whole. These trends hold for both the math and verbal portions of the SAT.

4.1 NAEP: Music

National Assessment of Educational Progress in music: 1971–1972 and 1978–1979

Selected characteristics of participants	Age 9			Age 13			Age 17[a]		
	Mean percentage correct		Mean change	Mean percentage correct		Mean change	Mean percentage correct		Mean change
	1971–72	1978–79		1971–72	1978–79		1971–72	1978–79	
All participants	53.6	50.3	-3.3	41.8	41.3	-0.5	45.7	43.2	-2.5
Region									
Northeast	56.5	51.7	-4.8	42.1	41.8	-0.4	46.6	43.3	-3.3
Southeast	51.0	47.2	-3.9	40.0	39.4	-0.7	43.8	41.3	-2.6
Central	55.0	52.0	-3.1	43.3	42.4	-0.9	47.3	44.1	-3.2
West	51.3	50.4	-1.0	41.3	41.6	+0.3	44.4	43.9	-0.5
Sex									
Male	52.8	49.9	-3.0	40.4	40.2	-0.2	44.4	41.6	-2.8
Female	54.3	50.8	-3.5	43.2	42.4	-0.8	46.9	44.6	-2.2
Race									
Black	43.3	41.0	-2.3	36.1	35.6	-0.4	38.1	36.5	-1.5
White	56.0	52.3	-3.6	42.9	42.4	-0.5	47.0	44.4	-2.6
Hispanic	45.1	42.8	-2.3	36.6	35.1	-1.5	36.4	36.4	0.0
Parental education									
Not high school graduate	48.1	44.2	-3.9	38.5	36.8	-1.7	40.2	37.3	-2.9
Graduated high school	53.5	50.5	-3.0	41.8	40.9	-0.9	45.0	41.1	-4.0
Post high school	58.4	54.6	-3.8	45.2	44.2	-1.0	49.2	46.5	-2.7
Size and type of community									
Extreme rural	51.7	45.8	-5.9	40.9	39.3	-1.6	43.4	40.4	-3.0
Low metropolitan	43.4	42.0	-1.4	36.5	35.1	-1.4	40.7	37.9	-2.8
High metropolitan	59.8	56.0	-3.8	45.2	45.5	+0.3	49.5	46.5	-3.0
Main big city	48.9	49.1	+0.2	40.8	40.3	-0.4	44.5	42.7	-1.8
Urban fringe	56.4	52.9	-3.6	42.4	43.2	+0.8	47.0	43.2	-3.8
Medium city	55.9	49.2	-6.8	41.7	40.0	-1.6	47.2	43.5	-3.6
Small place	53.2	50.2	-2.9	41.8	41.1	-0.7	44.8	43.3	-1.6

[a] All participants of this age were in school.

Note: The mean change is equal to the difference in the mean correct for each year but may differ in this table because of rounding.

Source: National Assessment of Educational Progress, *Music 1971–79: Results from the Second National Music Assessment*, 1981. Reprinted from: Grant, Vance W., and Elden, Leo J., *Digest of Education Statistics*, 1982 (Washington, DC: National Center for Education Statistics), p. 30.

National Assessment of Educational Progress in music: 1971–1972 and 1978–1979

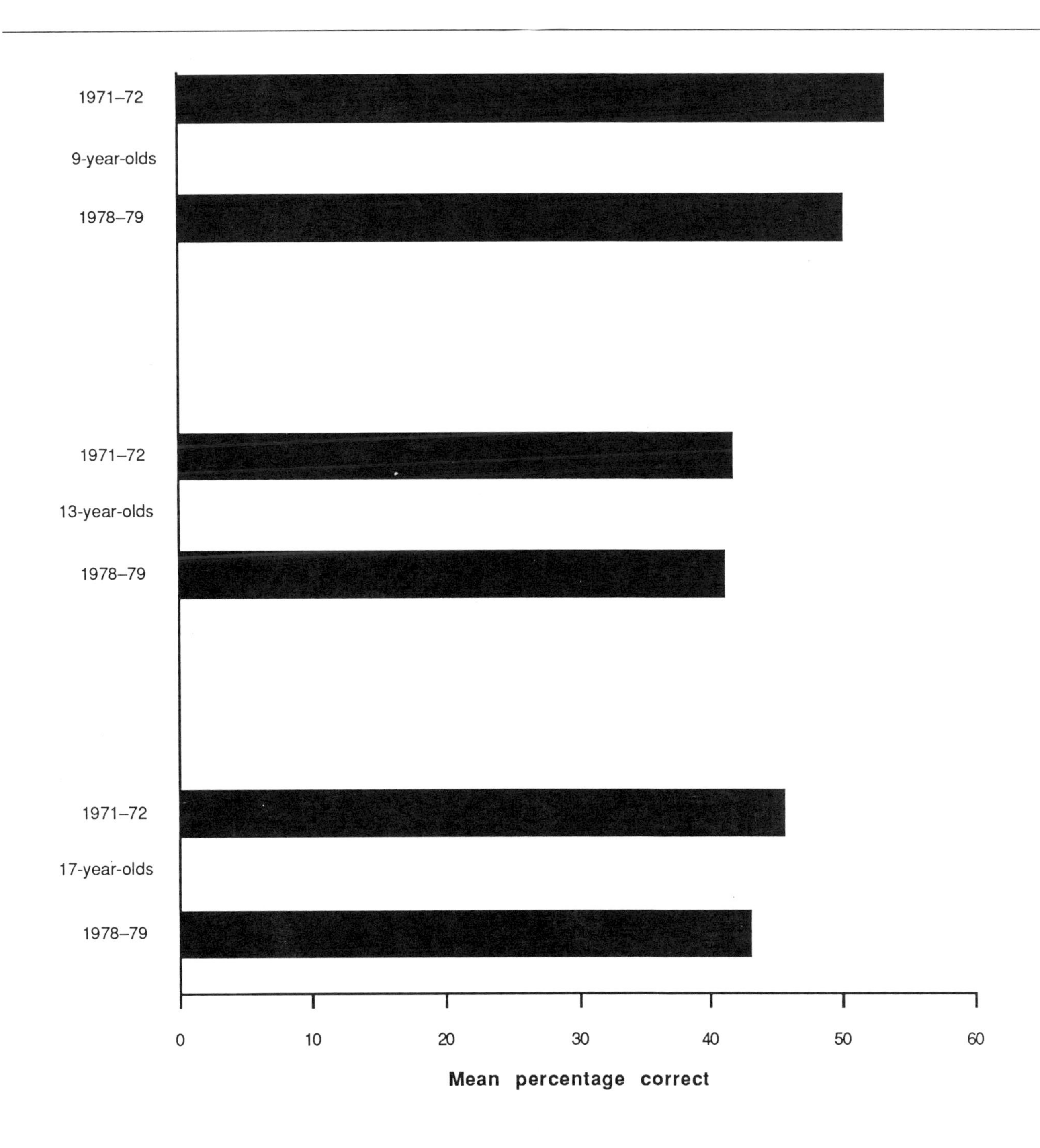

4.2 NAEP: Art

National Assessment of Educational Progress in art: 1974–1975 and 1978–1979

Selected characteristics of participants	Age 9			Age 13			Age 17[a]		
	Mean percentage correct		Mean change	Mean percentage correct		Mean change	Mean percentage correct		Mean change
	1971–72	1978–79		1971–72	1978–79		1971–72	1978–79	
All participants	36.9	37.6	0.7	49.9	47.7	-2.2	56.3	54.4	-1.9
Region									
Northeast	38.8	39.0	0.3	51.6	50.8	-0.8	58.0	55.6	-2.4
Southeast	33.9	36.0	2.1	46.8	44.6	-2.2	53.4	51.7	-1.7
Central	38.3	36.8	-1.5	51.8	47.4	-4.4	57.3	54.0	-3.3
West	35.8	38.3	2.4	48.7	47.6	-1.2	55.8	55.8	0.0
Sex									
Male	38.0	39.1	1.1	49.2	47.4	-1.8	55.0	53.1	-1.9
Female	35.8	36.0	0.3	50.5	48.0	-2.6	57.5	55.5	-2.0
Race									
Black	33.5	33.7	0.3	44.2	41.2	-2.9	48.5	48.3	-0.2
White	37.7	38.4	0.8	51.2	49.1	-2.1	57.6	55.3	-2.2
Hispanic	34.1	34.1	0.0	43.2	44.0	0.7	51.3	50.5	-0.8
Parental education									
Not high school graduate	33.6	34.8	1.2	44.7	43.5	-1.2	50.7	48.9	-1.7
Graduated high school	36.4	37.6	1.3	48.7	46.3	-2.4	54.8	51.8	-3.0
Post high school	41.1	42.1	1.0	54.7	52.0	-2.7	60.4	57.8	-2.6
Size and type of community									
Extreme rural	35.0	35.0	0.1	45.7	45.0	-0.6	55.1	48.3	-6.8
Low metropolitan	33.7	34.8	1.1	47.2	43.1	-4.1	53.3	50.7	-2.6
High metropolitan	42.3	41.7	-0.6	55.4	51.1	-4.3	61.3	59.2	-2.6
Main big city	35.8	36.9	1.1	48.2	47.1	-1.1	55.9	54.2	-1.7
Urban fringe	40.3	38.3	-2.0	53.4	47.4	-5.9	58.0	56.2	-1.7
Medium city	36.2	37.5	1.3	49.2	48.0	-1.2	56.0	55.2	-0.9
Small place	35.5	37.5	2.0	48.8	47.8	-0.9	55.5	53.1	-2.4

[a] All participants of this age were in school.

Source: National Assessment of Educational Progress, *Art and Young Americans, 1974–79: Results from the Second National Art Assessment*, 1981.

Note: The mean change is equal to the difference in the mean correct for each year but may differ in this table because of rounding. Reprinted from: Grant, Vance W., and Elden, Leo J., *Digest of Education Statistics*, 1982 (Washington, DC: National Center for Education Statistics), p. 31.

National Assessment of Educational Progress in art: 1974–1975 and 1978–1979

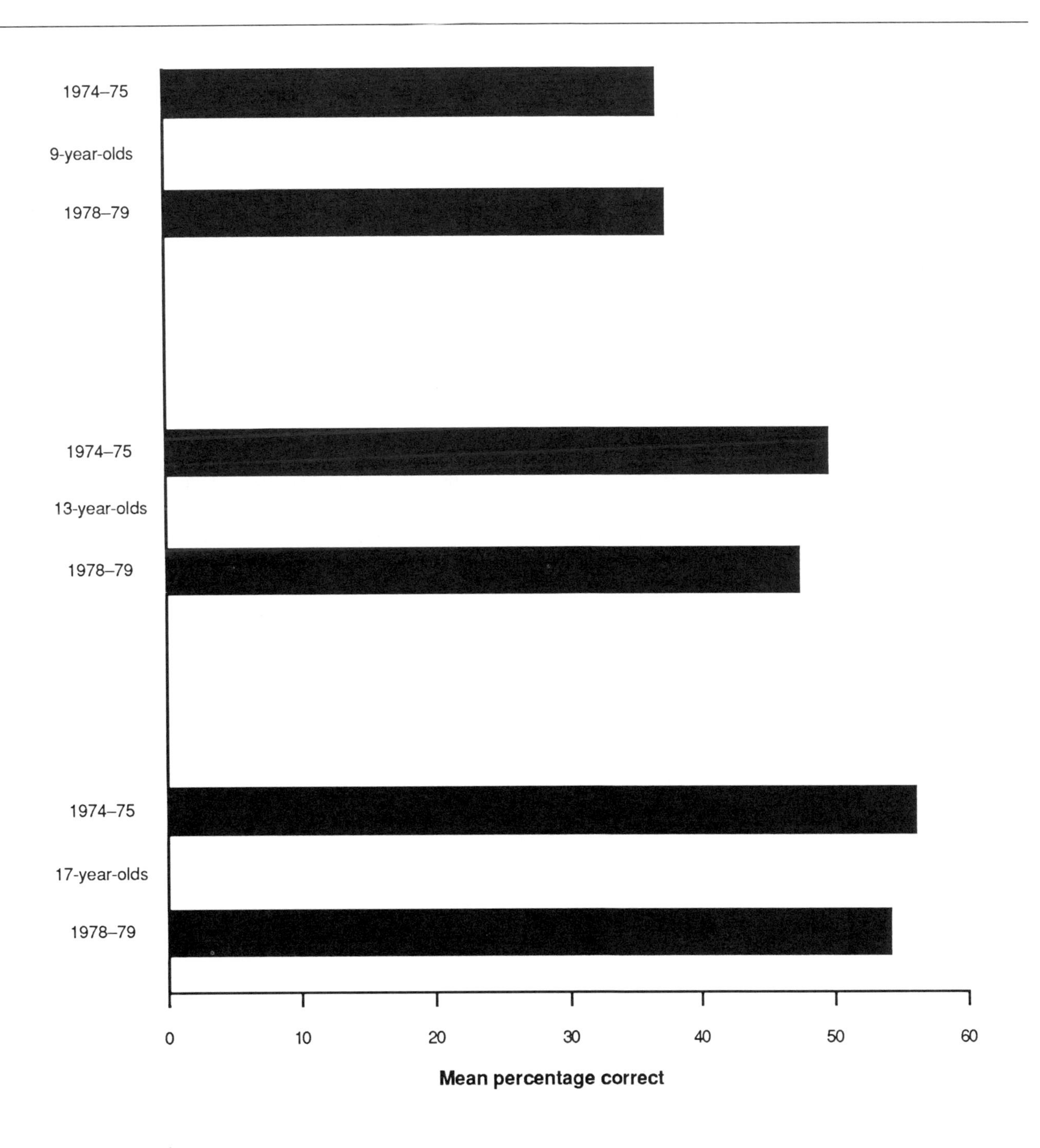

4.3 SAT scores for arts students

SAT scores for students having coursework/experience in arts education: 1987–1989

	Participation percentage[a]			Verbal mean scores			Math mean scores		
	87	88	89	87	88	89	87	88	89
Title of course									
Acting/play production	21	22	22	469	465	465	497	496	497
Art history/appreciation	19	20	22	445	442	441	479	481	482
Dance	12	12	12	437	433	432	468	469	469
Drama appreciation	12	13	13	457	453	454	482	483	485
Music appreciation	18	18	18	457	455	454	493	494	495
Music performance	38	38	38	450	447	446	490	490	491
Photography/film	14	15	15	449	446	446	489	490	492
Studio art and design	17	19	21	446	444	443	484	485	488
No coursework	27	25	21	415	412	408	471	470	467
All students				430	428	427	476	476	476

[a] This is the percentage of students each year who indicated participation on the Student Descriptive Questionnaire. Because not all students responded to all items on the questionnaire, equal percentages do not represent equal numbers of students taking individual courses but instead represent general rates of participation.

Notes: Because of the students' high response rate (approximately 95 percent) to the Student Descriptive Questionnaire and because studies document the accuracy of self-reported student information, this table can be considered nearly a complete and accurate description of the tested population. Total SAT takers were 1,080,426 for 1987, 1,134,364 for 1988, and 1,088,223 for 1989.

Sources: The College Board, *1987 Profile of SAT and Achievement Test Takers*, College Entrance Examination Board, pp. 1 and 3, *1988 Profile of SAT and Achievement Test Takers*, College Entrance Examination Board, pp. 1 and 3, *1989 Profile of SAT and Achievement Test Takers*, College Entrance Examination Board, pp. 1 and 3. Used by permission.

SAT scores for students having coursework/exposure in arts education: 1989

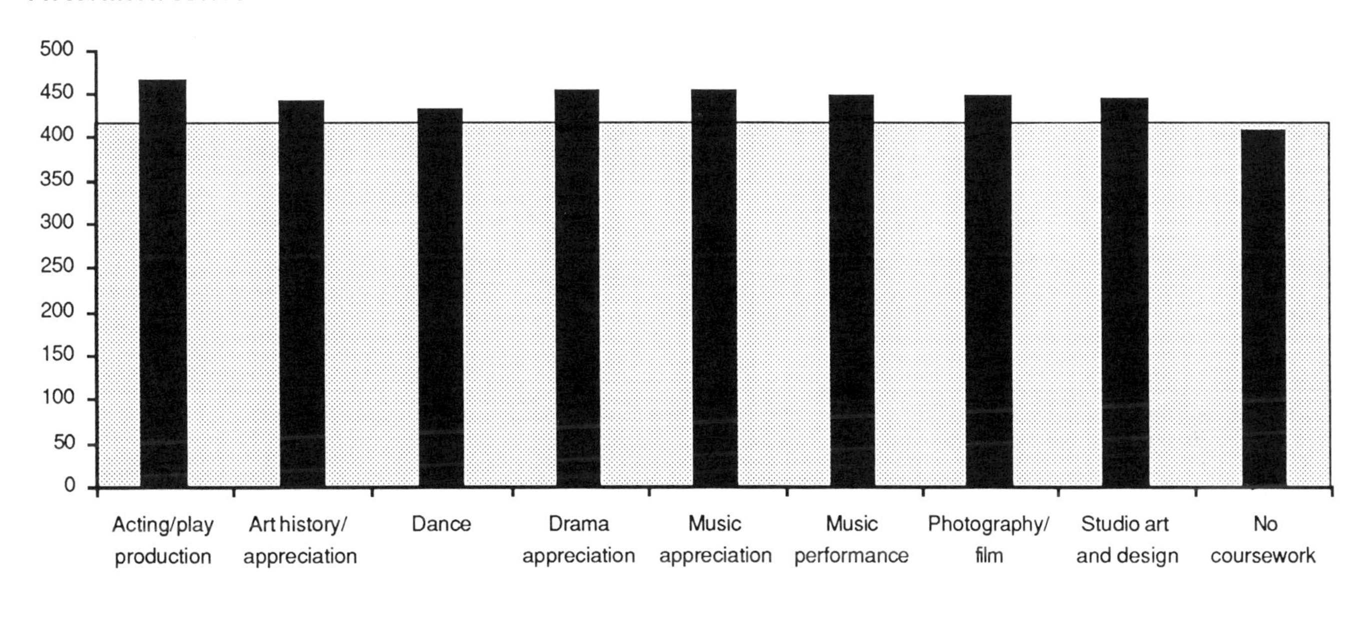

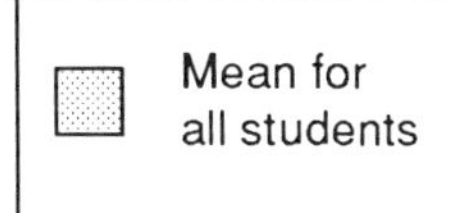

Math mean scores

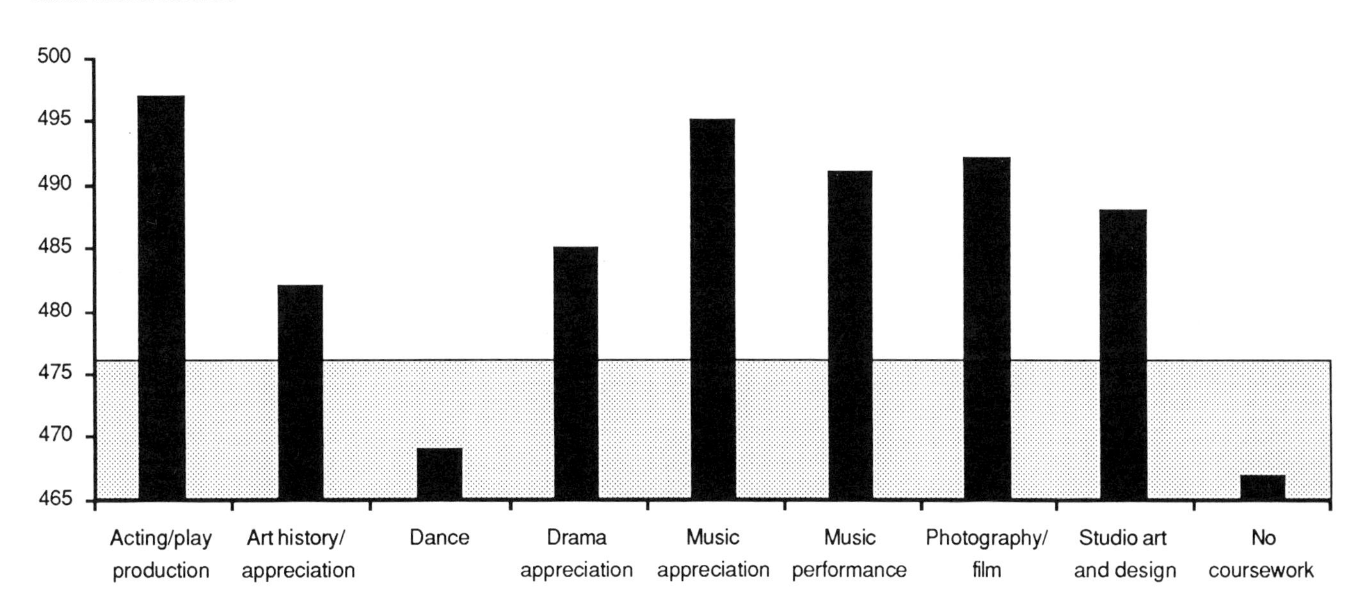

4.4 SAT scores: Years of arts study

Student SAT scores by years of high school arts study: 1987–1989

	Participation percentage[a]			Verbal mean scores			Math mean scores		
	87	88	89	87	88	89	87	88	89
More than 4 years	7	7	7	455	453	454	491	492	493
4 years	10	10	11	455	453	452	489	491	490
3 or 3.5 years	8	9	9	434	433	432	469	471	472
2 or 2.5 years	14	14	15	432	430	429	472	473	474
1 or 1.5 years	25	28	31	428	427	426	475	476	479
Less than 1 year	36	32	27	425	422	420	479	477	475
All students				430	428	427	476	476	476

[a] This is the percentage of students who provided answers for this item on the Student Descriptive Questionnaire.

Notes: Because of the students' high response rate (approximately 95 percent) to the Student Descriptive Questionnaire and because studies document the accuracy of self-reported student information, this table can be considered nearly a complete and accurate description of the tested population. Total SAT takers were 1,080,426 for 1987, 1,134,364 for 1988, and 1,088,223 for 1989.

Sources: The College Board, *1987 Profile of SAT and Achievement Test Takers*, College Entrance Examination Board, pp. 1 and 3, *1988 Profile of SAT and Achievement Test Takers*, College Entrance Examination Board, pp. 1 and 3, *1989 Profile of SAT and Achievement Test Takers*, College Entrance Examination Board, pp. 1 and 3. Used by permission.

Student SAT scores by years of high school arts study: 1989

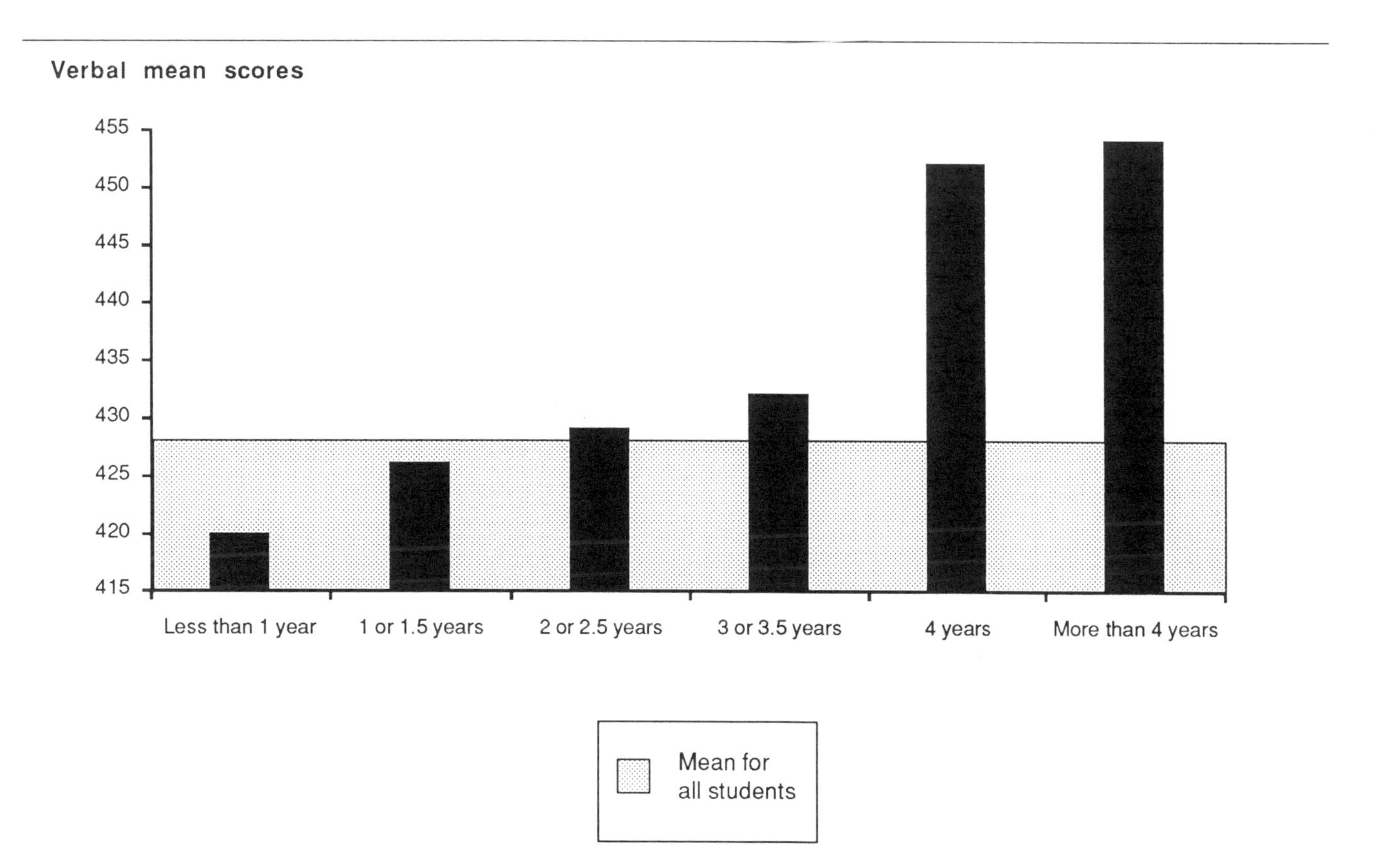

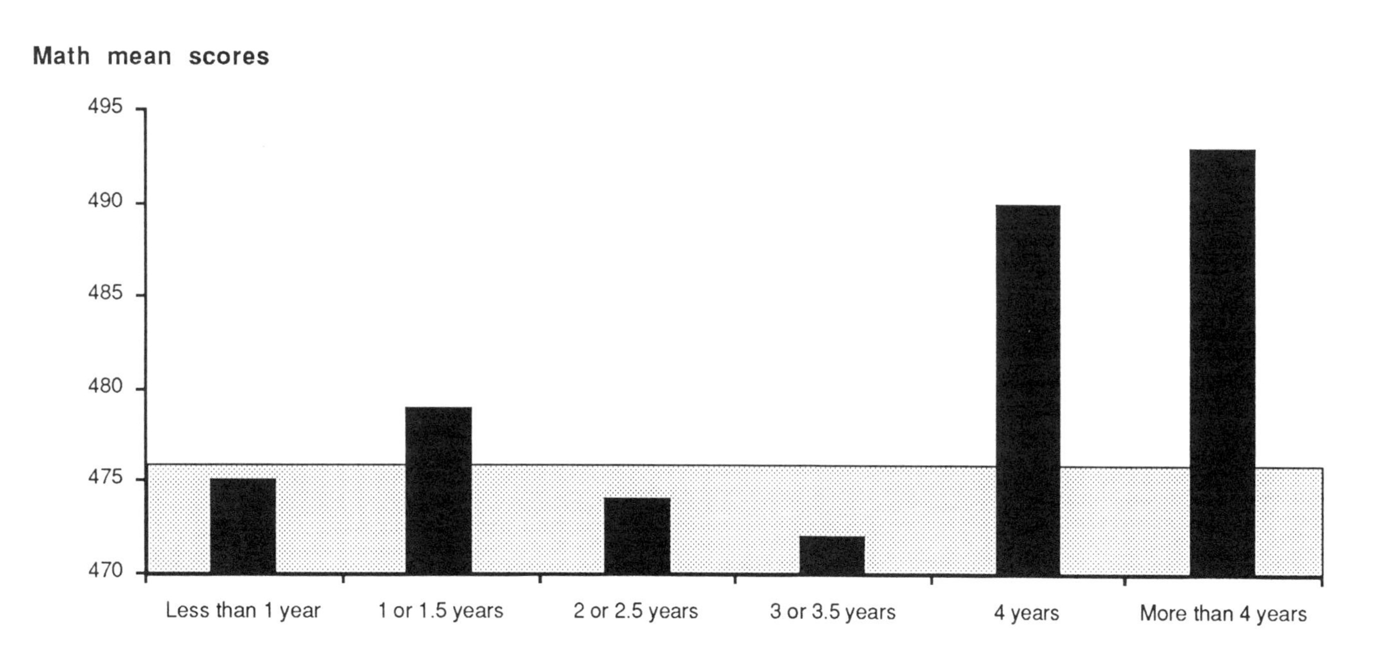

4.5 Graduate Record Exam

Changes in performance on Graduate Record Examinations

Test[a]	Change in standard deviation units	
	Long-term (1964–1987)	Short-term (1976–1987)
Mathematics	0.37	0.12
Physics	.13	-.10
Quantitative	.12	.26
Engineering	.01	.23
Chemistry	.01	-.01
Biology	-.01	-.08
Computer science	NA	-.07
Econornics	-.10	.07
Education	-.18	.13
Psychology	-.21	.04
Music	**-.22**	**.05**
Geology[b]	-.31	-.08
Verbal	-.42	-.10
Literature in English	-.67	-.06
History	-.74	-.08
Sociology	-1.04	-.22
Political science	-1.14	-.23

[a] Quantitative and Verbal are general examinations, while all others are tests in specific areas.

[b] The long-term trend for the geology area test was calculated for the period 1967–87.

Note: NA = not applicable; tests in this area began in 1976. A change in the range of -0.10 to +0.10 is really no change. Changes exceeding -0.4 or +0.4 are large.

Source: U.S. Department of Education, Office of Research, *The Standardized Test Scores of College Graduates, 1964–1982*, 1985; and special tabulations. As printed in *1988 Education Indicators*, U.S. Department of Education, Office of Educational Research and Improvement, National Center for Education Statistics, Washington, DC, September 1988, Joyce D. Stern (editor) and Marjorie O. Chandles (associate editor), p. 251.

Changes in performance on Graduate Record Examinations

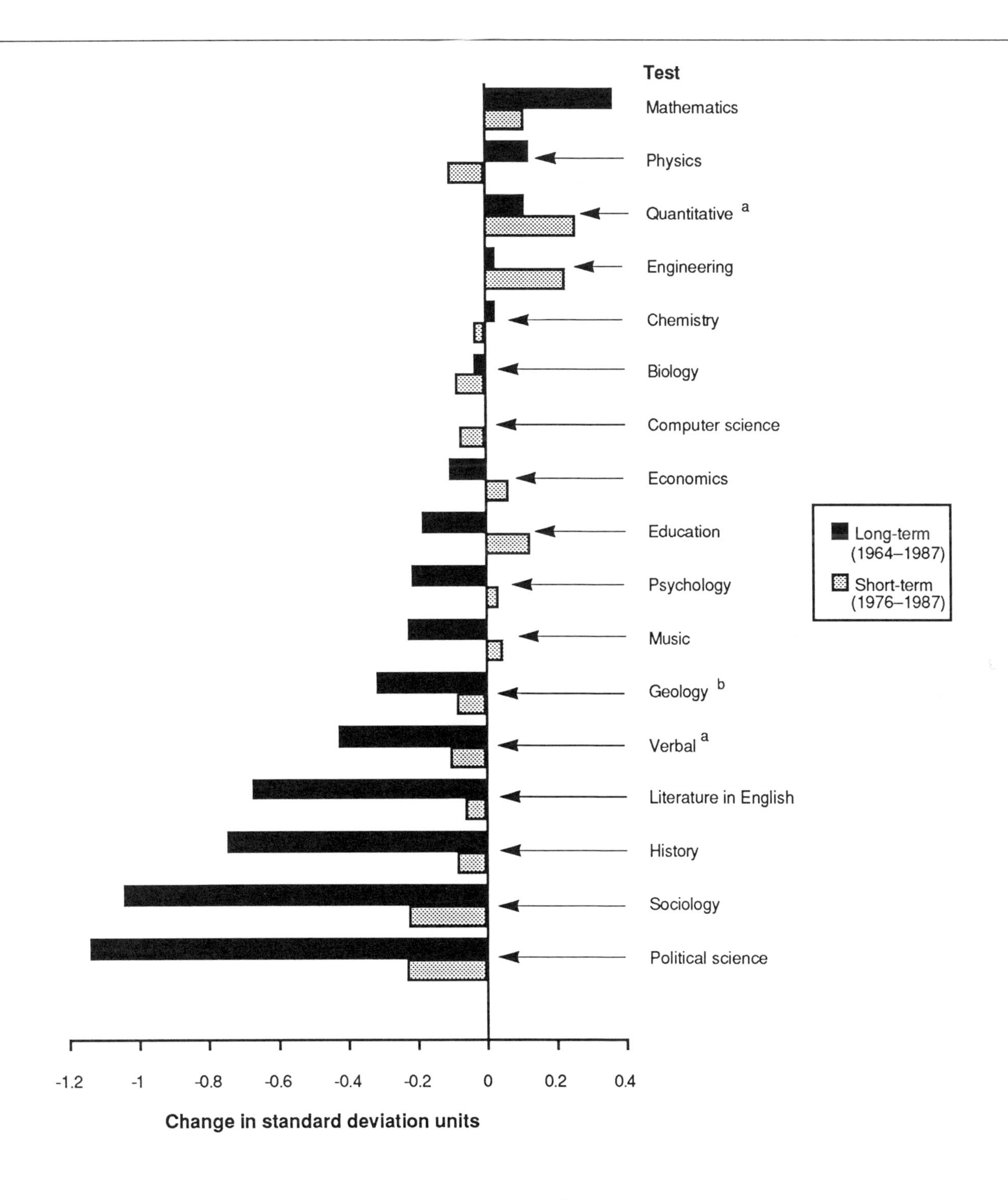

[a] Quantitative and Verbal are general examinations, while all others are tests in specific areas.

[b] The long-term trend for the geology test area was calculated for the period 1967–87.

Chapter 5

Secondary School Offerings and Enrollments

The enrollment and course offerings data for 1972–1973 and 1981–1982 in this chapter are based on reported course enrollments and student transcripts. The 1986–1987 enrollment data are based on district level school officials' estimated percentage of student enrollment in arts courses. The extracurricular information is based on student-reported data.

5.1 Secondary enrollment: Selected years

Public secondary day school pupils enrolled in specific subjects in selected years

Specific subject	1890	1900	1910	1915	1922	1928	1934	1949
Total enrollment	202,963	519,251	739,143	1,165,495	2,155,460	2,896,630	4,496,514	5,399,452
English	—	38.5	57.1	58.4	76.7	93.1	90.5	92.9
Journalism	—	—	—	—	0.1	0.2	0.7	1.9
Radio speaking and broadcasting	—	—	—	—	—	—	—	0.1
United States history	27.3[a]	38.2[a]	55.0[a]	50.5[a]	15.3	17.9	17.3	22.8
English history	—	—	—	—	2.9	0.9	0.5	b
World history	—	—	—	—	—	6.1	11.9	16.2
Civil government	—	21.7	15.6	15.7	19.3	6.6	6.0	8.0
Community government	—	—	—	—	—	13.4	10.4	c
Geography	—	—	—	—	—	0.3	2.1	5.6
Problems of democracy	—	—	—	—	—	1.0	3.5	5.2
Economics	—	—	—	—	4.8	5.1	4.9	4.7
Sociology	—	—	—	—	2.4	2.7	2.5	3.4
Psychology	—	2.4	1.0	1.2	0.9	1.0	0.3	0.9
Consumer education	—	—	—	—	—	—	—	0.7
General science	—	—	—	—	18.3	17.5	17.8	20.8
Biology	—	—	1.1	6.9	8.8	13.6	14.6	18.4
Botany	—	—	15.8	9.1	3.8	1.6	0.9	0.1
Physiology	—	27.4	15.3	9.5	5.1	2.7	1.8	1.0
Zoology	—	—	6.9	3.2	1.5	0.8	0.6	0.1
Earth science	—	29.8	21.0	15.3	4.5	2.8	1.7	0.4
Chemistry	10.1	7.7	6.9	7.4	7.4	7.1	7.6	7.6
Physics	22.8	19.0	14.6	14.2	8.9	6.8	6.3	5.4
Algebra	45.4	56.3	56.9	48.8	40.2	35.2	30.4	26.8
General mathematics	—	—	—	—	12.4	7.9	7.4	13.1
Geometry	21.3	27.4	30.9	26.5	22.7	19.8	17.1	12.8
Trigonometry	—	1.9	1.9	1.5	1.5	1.3	1.3	2.0
Spanish	—	—	0.7	2.7	11.3	9.4	6.2	8.2
Latin	34.7	50.6	49.0	37.3	27.5	22.0	16.0	7.8
French	5.8	7.8	9.9	8.8	15.5	14.0	10.9	4.7
German	10.5	14.3	23.7	24.4	0.6	1.8	2.4	0.8
Italian	—	—	—	—	b	0.1	0.2	0.3
Portuguese	—	—	—	—	—	—	—	b
Russian	—	—	—	—	—	—	—	b
Industrial subjects	—	—	—	11.2	13.7	13.5	21.0	26.6
General business training	—	—	—	—	—	3.0	6.2	5.2
Business arithmetic	—	—	—	—	1.5	6.9	4.9	4.6
Bookkeeping	—	—	—	3.4	12.	10.7	9.9	8.7
Typewriting	—	—	—	—	13.1	15.2	16.7	22.5
Shorthand	—	—	—	—	8.9	8.7	9.0	7.8
Business law	—	—	—	—	0.9	2.6	3.2	2.4
Business English	—	—	—	—	—	0.5	0.9	1.0
Economic geography	—	—	—	—	1.7	4.8	4.0	1.7
Office practice	—	—	—	—	0.4	1.5	1.8	2.0
Retailing	—	—	—	—	—	—	—	0.5
Salesmanship and advertising	—	—	—	—	0.3	0.4	0.7	1.0
Cooperative office training	—	—	—	—	—	—	—	0.4
Cooperative store training	—	—	—	—	—	—	—	0.3
Home economics	—	—	3.8	12.9	14.3	16.5	16.7	24.2
Agriculture	—	—	4.7	7.2	5.1	3.7	3.6	6.7
Physical education	—	—	—	—	5.7	15.0	50.7	69.4
Music	—	—	—	31.5	25.3	26.0	25.5	30.1
Art	—	—	—	22.9	14.7	11.7	8.7	9.0
Teacher training	—	—	—	—	1.0	1.8	0.1	b

[a] Includes ancient history and medieval and modern history.

[b] Less that 0.05 percent or fewer than 1 pupil in 2,000.

[c] Comparable data for 1949 not available.

Note: — indicates not a separate category. Figures cover enrollment in the last four years of school, for school year ending in the year indicated.

Methodological note: For 1910–1934, the percentages are based on the number of pupils enrolled in the last four years in all schools that returned usable questionnaires. For 1890, 1900, and 1949, the figures are based on the total number of pupils enrolled in the last fours years of all schools. The source states that "when necessary, the subjects reported in previous surveys were analyzed, and appropriate components were either recombined, separately listed, or eliminated (with corresponding changes in the number and percentage enrolled) in a manner to yield as close comparability as possible with the data in the current (1948–49) survey."

Source: Office of Education, *Biennial Survey of Education in the United States, 1948–1950*, Washington, DC. As included in U.S. Bureau of Census, *Historical Statistics of the United States, Colonial Times to 1970*, Washington, DC, 1975, Series H 262–315. Reprinted from: Westat, Inc. (under contract to the National Endowment for the Arts), *A Sourcebook of Arts Statistics: 1987*, Rockville, MD, April 1988, p. 145.

5.1a Secondary enrollment: Selected years

Public secondary day school pupils enrolled in specific subjects in selected years

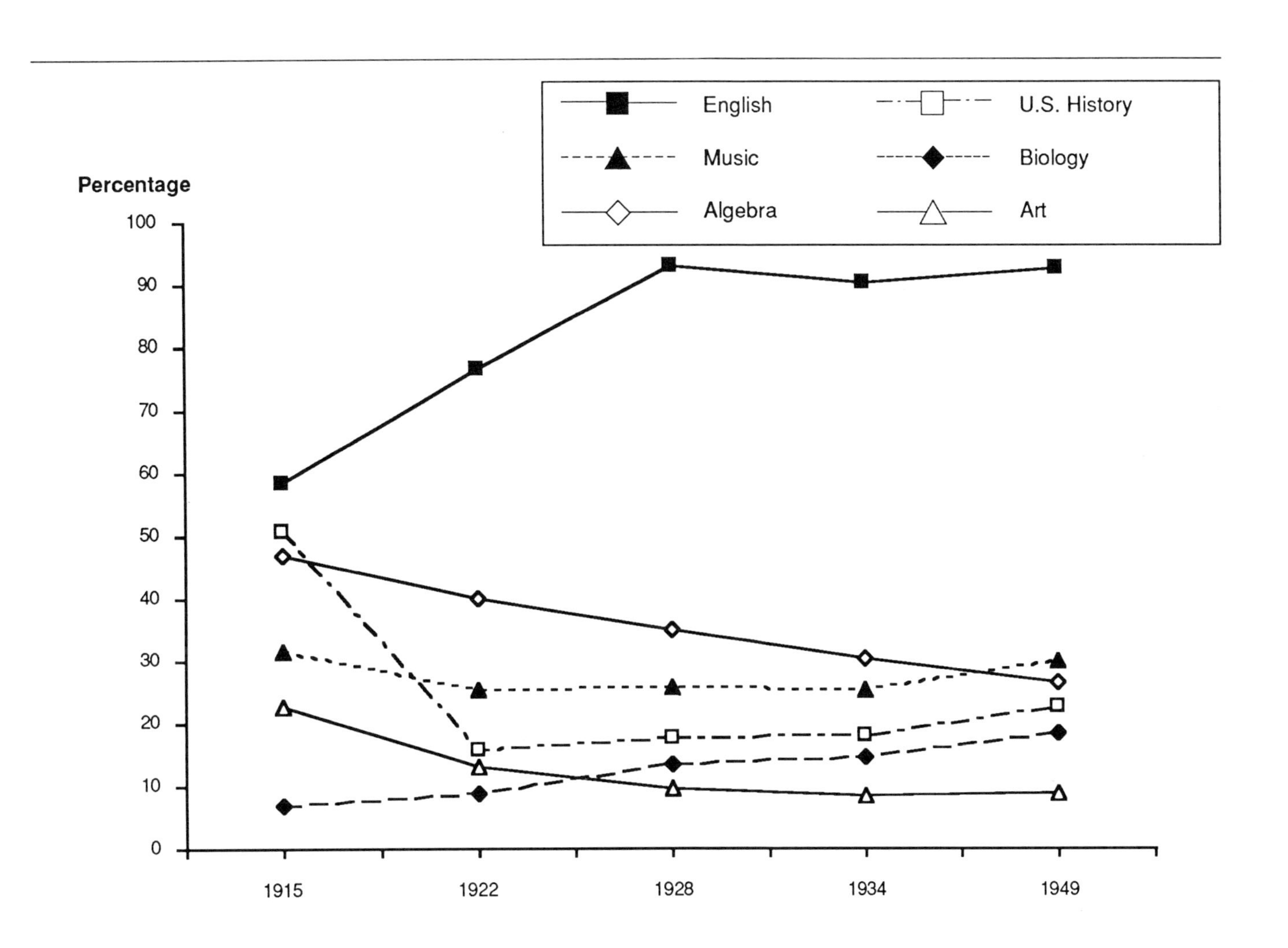

5.2 Secondary enrollment: 1973 and 1982

Number of students enrolled in selected subject areas in public secondary schools: 1972–1973 and 1981–1982

Subject area	1972–73[a] Number (in thousands)	1972–73[a] Percentage	1981–82[b] Number (in thousands)	1981–82[b] Percentage	Percentage change, 1972–73 to 1981–82
Total enrollment, Grades 9–12	11,975	100.0	12,661	100.0	5.7
English language arts	15,605	130.3	17,716	139.9	13.5
Health and physical education	8,679	72.5	11,859	93.7	36.6
Social sciences	11,710	97.8	15,008	118.5	28.2
Mathematics	6,619	55.3	9,850	77.8	48.8
Natural sciences	6,119	51.1	8,278	65.4	35.3
Music	**3,004**	**25.1**	**2,733**	**21.6**	**-9.0**
Business	5,763	48.1	5,864	46.4	1.9
Industrial arts	2,903	24.2	2,980	23.5	2.7
Home economics	2,439	20.4	3,024	23.9	24.0
Foreign languages	3,067	25.6	2,953	23.3	-3.7
Art	**2,143**	**17.9**	**3,061**	**24.2**	**42.8**
Agriculture	322	2.7	420	3.3	30.4
Vocational trade and industrial education	447	3.7	1,874	14.8	319.2
Safety and driver's education	3,297	27.5	2,026	16.0	-38.6
R.O.T.C.	142	1.2	172	1.4	21.1
Computer science	NA	NA	344	2.7	NA
Allied health	NA	NA	80	0.6	NA

[a] Data have been revised since originally published to make them more comparable with the figures of 1981–82.

[b] These estimates are based on student transcript data.

Note: NA indicates data either not reported, not available, or not applicable. Percentages in columns 3 and 5 may exceed 100.0 because a student may have been enrolled in more than one course within a subject area during the school year. Data are based upon sample surveys and may differ somewhat from those reported elsewhere.

Source: U.S. Department of Education, National Center for Education Statistics, *A Trend Study of High School Offerings and Enrollments: 1972–73 and 1981–82.* As included in U.S. Department of Education, Center for Education Statistics, *Digest of Education Statistics: 1985–86,* U.S. Government Printing Office, Washington, DC, February 1986, p. 41.

Percentage change in student enrollments in selected subject areas in public secondary schools: 1972–1973 to 1981–1982

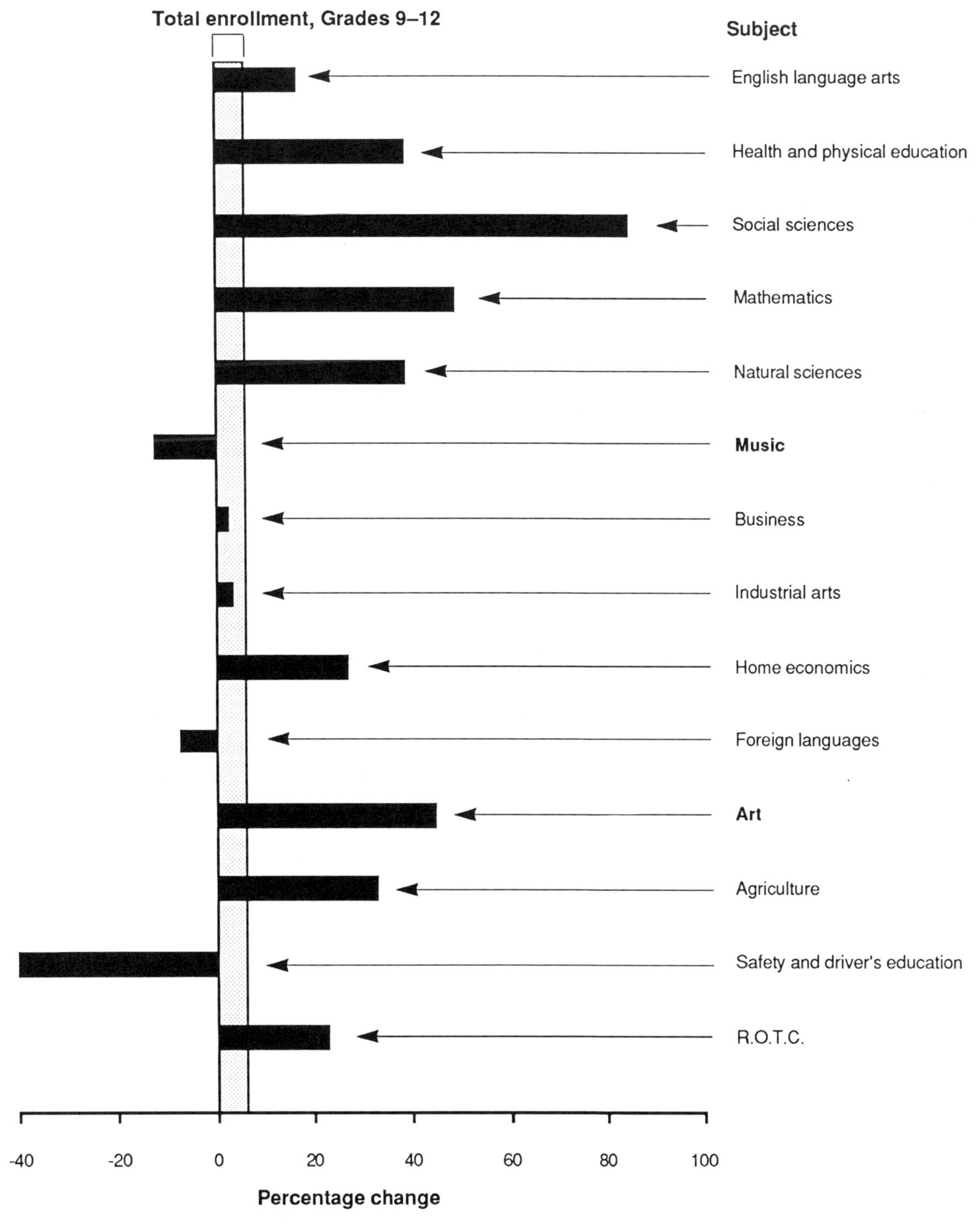

Note: Change in Vocational education and Industrial arts enrollment not shown due to limitations of chart size.

5.3 Secondary enrollment: Music

Offerings and enrollments in specific music courses in public secondary schools: 1973 and 1982

Course	Number of schools offering course	As a percentage of all secondary schools	Total enrollment in course (thousands)	As a percentage of total secondary enrollment
1973				
General music	2,173	14.2	206	1.7
Music appreciation	3,211	21.0	119	1.0
Theory and harmony/composition	3,455	22.6	60	0.5
Choir, chorus, glee club	12,106	79.1	1,240	10.4
Instrumental music	2,657	17.4	150	1.2
Band (marching, concert, stage)	12,598	82.3	1,065	8.9
Orchestra	2,969	19.4	102	0.9
Small instrumental ensembles	2,179	14.2	63	0.5
Any music course	13,437	87.9	3,004	25.1
1982				
General music	1,662	10.6	61	0.5
Music appreciation	3,953	25.2	99	0.8
Theory and harmony/composition	5,420	34.6	72	0.6
Choir, chorus, glee club	12,340	78.8	1,061	8.4
Instrumental music	5,395	34.4	190	1.5
Band (marching, concert, stage)	13,574	86.6	1,111	8.8
Orchestra	2,886	18.4	86	0.7
Small instrumental ensembles	1,970	12.6	52	0.4
Any music course	14,566	93.0	2,733	21.6

Note: For 1973, total U.S. secondary schools = 15,306; total secondary enrollment = 11,974,683. For 1982, total U.S. secondary schools = 15,667; total secondary enrollment = 12,660,537.

Source: National Center for Education Statistics, *A Trend Study of High School Offerings and Enrollments: 1972–73 and 1981–82*, U.S. Government Printing Office, Washington, DC, pp. 39, 55.

Compiler's note: These data are based on enrollments reported by school districts in 1973 and an analysis of high school transcripts in 1982. They are not directly comparable to enrollment data presented in Table 5.7, which asked district superintendents to estimate what percentage of students participated in each art.

Percentage of public secondary school students enrolled in music: 1973 and 1982

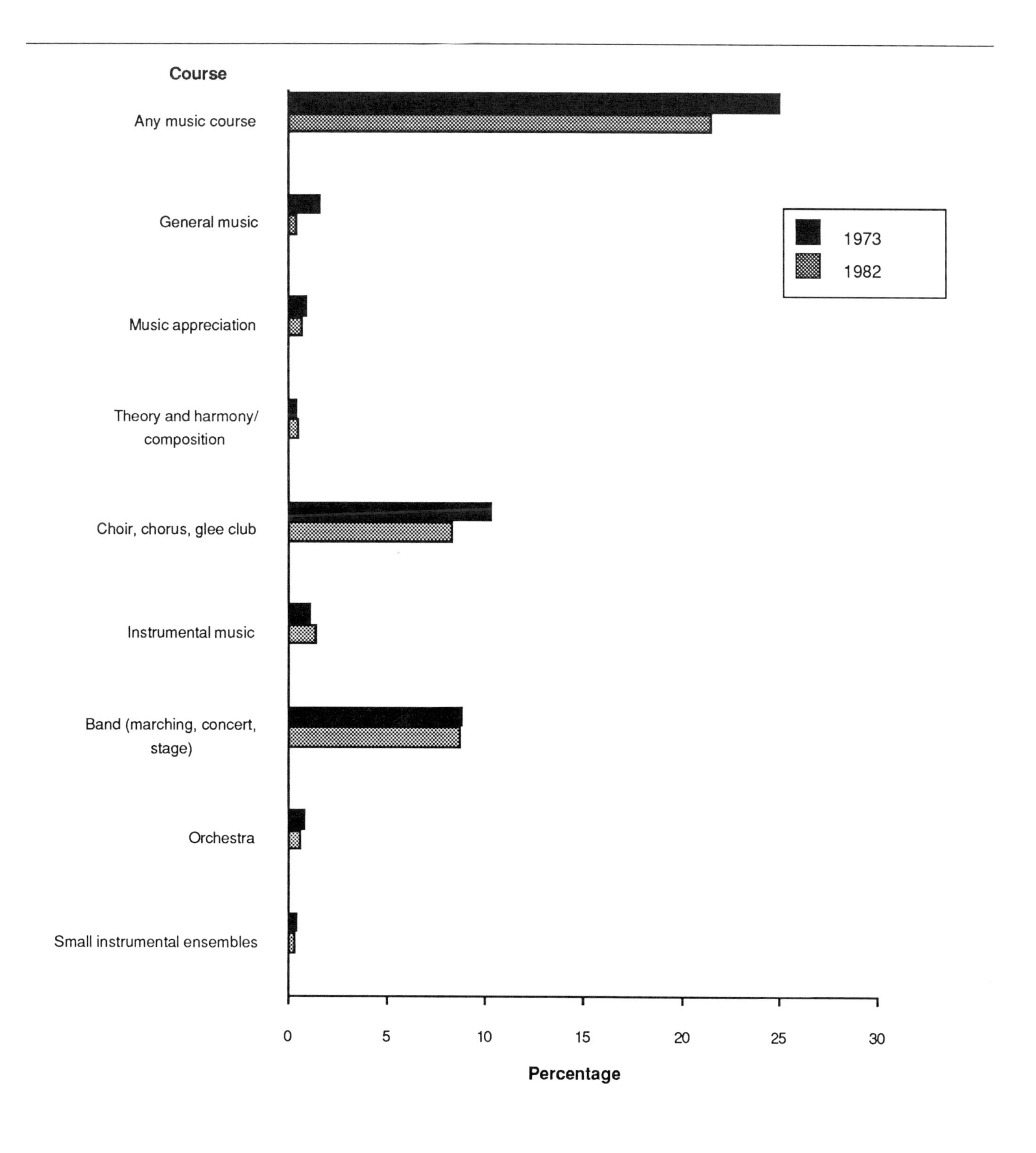

5.4 Secondary enrollment: Art

Offerings and enrollments in specific art courses in public secondary schools: 1973 and 1982

Course	Number of schools offering course	As a percentage of all secondary schools	Total enrollment in course (thousands)	As a percentage of total secondary enrollment
1973				
Art I	9,296	60.7	767	6.4
Art II	6,938	45.3	266	2.2
Art III/IV and art studio	5,672	37.1	203	1.7
Art appreciation/history	1,311	8.6	88	0.7
Design, commercial/industrial	1,834	12.0	80	0.7
Drafting/drawing, grade 9-12[a]	5,238	34.2	278	2.3
Drawing, mechanical, grade 9-12[a]	4,570	29.9	243	2.0
Graphics	920	6.0	29	0.2
Crafts	1,855	12.1	162	1.4
Crafts, grade 9-12[a]	963	6.3	69	0.6
Jewelry and metalwork	1,051	6.9	65	0.5
Jewelry/art metals[a]	528	3.4	29	0.2
Pottery and ceramics	2,485	16.2	178	1.5
Painting/drawing/design	3,033	19.6	204	1.7
Photography/filmmaking	983	6.4	63	0.5
Graphic arts, grade 9-12[a]	1,723	11.3	99	0.8
Photography[a]	840	5.5	42	0.4
Printing/photolithography/graphic communications[a]	505	3.3	24	0.2
Sculpture	1,091	7.1	37	0.3
Any art course[b]	11,329	74.0	2,143	17.9
1982				
Art I	12,129	77.4	1,049	8.3
Art II	7,353	46.9	271	2.1
Art III/IV and art studio	4,534	28.9	104	0.8
Art appreciation/history	2,075	13.2	70	0.6
Design, commercial/industrial	8,586	54.8	363	2.9
Graphics	5,225	33.3	256	2.0
Crafts	2,423	15.5	83	0.7
Jewelry and metalworks	1,542	9.8	65	0.5
Pottery and ceramics	4,516	28.8	272	2.2
Painting/drawing/design	5,647	36.0	382	3.0
Photography/filmmaking	2,213	14.1	90	0.7
Sculpture	2,893	18.5	56	0.4
Any art course[b]	14,034	89.6	3,061	24.2

[a] These categories were extracted from table "Industrial art 1973" in the original source. The 1982 tabulations, in the original source and in this table, incorporated these data into the table "Art 1982."

[b] The categories marked as note a are not included in the 1973 "Any art course." Therefore these categories are not comparable.

Note: For 1973, total U.S. secondary schools = 15,306; total secondary enrollment = 11,974,683. For 1982, total U.S. secondary schools = 15,667; total secondary enrollment = 12,660,537.

Source: National Center for Education Statistics, *A Trend Study of High School Offerings and Enrollments: 1972–73 and 1981–82*, U.S. Government Printing Office, Washington, DC, pp. 31, 37, 47.

Percentage of public secondary school students enrolled in selected art courses: 1973 and 1982

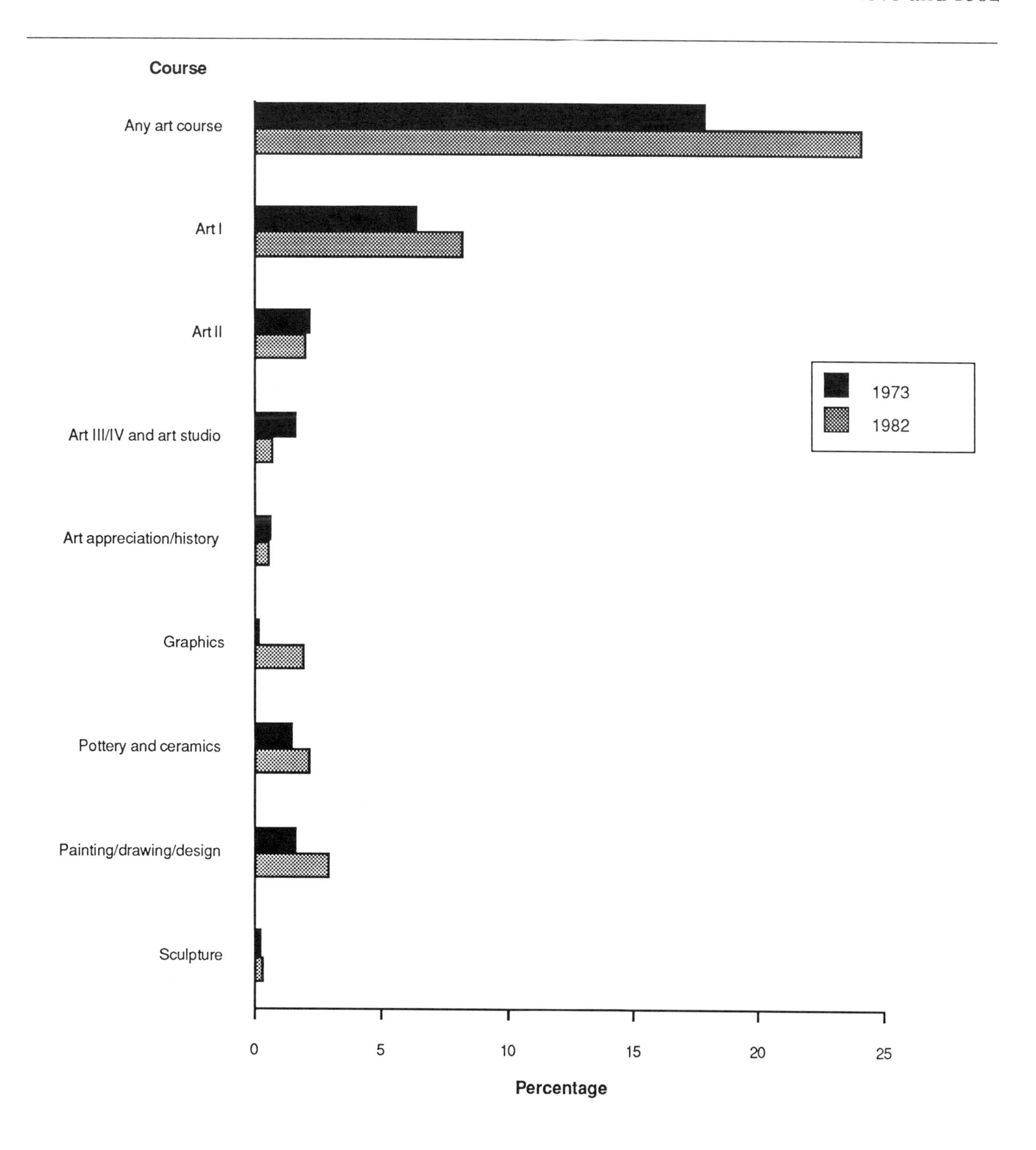

5.5 Secondary enrollment: Dance and drama

Offerings and enrollments in specific dance and drama courses in public secondary schools: 1973 and 1982

Course	Number of schools offering course	As a percentage of all secondary schools	Total enrollment in course (thousands)	As a percentage of total secondary enrollment
1973				
English language arts				
Creative writing	4,717	30.8	253	2.1
Radio/TV and film	1,294	8.5	130	1.1
Introduction to theater/drama	4,866	31.8	236	2.0
Acting/play production/creative dramatics	2,206	14.4	122	1.0
Health and physical education				
Dance, rhythm, and dramatic events	179	1.2	30	0.3
1982				
English language arts				
Creative writing	5,236	33.4	211	1.7
Radio/TV and film	4,903	31.3	287	2.3
Introduction to theater/drama	4,461	28.5	142	1.1
Acting/play production/creative dramatics	5,612	35.8	260	2.1
Health and physical education				
Dance, rhythm, and dramatic events	1,272	8.1	59	0.5

Note: Totals for these arts are not available because they were included as part of the English language arts and health and physical education groupings. For 1973, total U.S. secondary schools = 15,306; total secondary enrollment = 11,974,683. For 1982, total U.S. secondary schools = 15,667; total secondary enrollment = 12,660,537.

Source: National Center for Education Statistics, *A Trend Study of High School Offerings and Enrollments: 1972–73 and 1981–82*, U.S. Government Printing Office, Washington, DC, pp. 33, 35, 49, 51.

Percentage of public secondary school students enrolled in selected communications, dance, and drama courses: 1973 and 1982

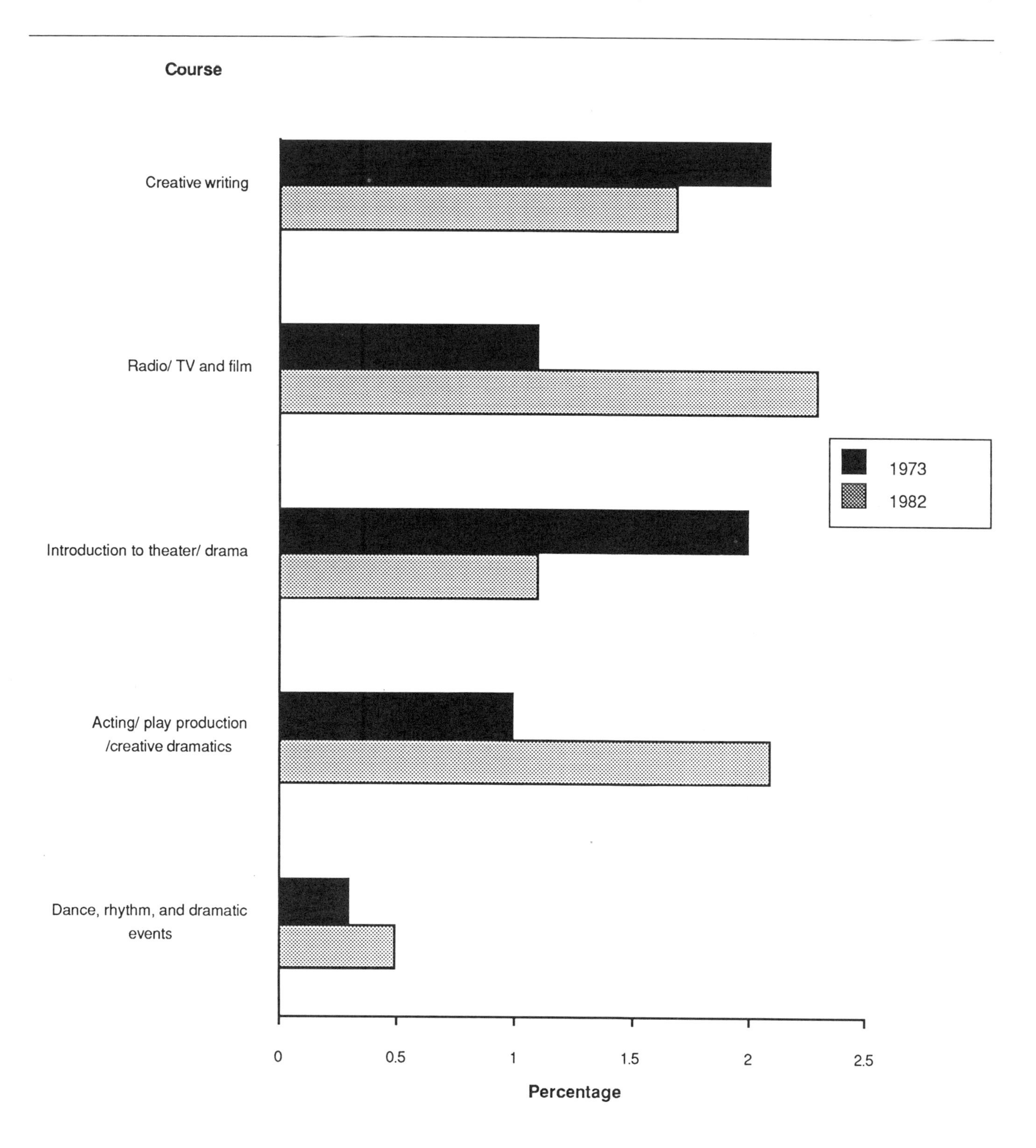

5.6 Offerings and enrollments: Recent changes

Changes in senior high arts courses offered, and enrollment in the last five years: 1986–1987

District characteristic	Changes in the last 5 years (percentages)					
	Number of arts courses offered			Enrollment in arts courses		
	Increased	Stayed about the same	Decreased	Increased	Stayed about the same	Decreased
	(Percentage of districts)					
All districts	37	52	10	39	40	21
Enrollment size						
Less than 2,500	36	55	9	37	42	21
2,500 to 9,999	42	47	11	47	34	18
10,000 or more	35	44	21	39	31	29
Metropolitan status						
Urban	24	45	32	21	52	27
Suburban	36	50	14	42	35	22
Rural	38	54	8	39	42	20
Geographic region[a]						
Northeast	53	39	9	51	33	16
Central	27	63	10	30	46	24
Southeast	44	48	8	49	37	13
West	39	47	14	41	37	22

[a] See Appendix for states in each geographic region.

Note: Percentages may not total to 100 because of rounding.

Source: Public School District Policies and Practices in Selected Aspects of Arts and Humanities Instruction (Washington, DC: U.S. Department of Education Center for Education Statistics), p. 17.

Changes in senior high arts courses offered, and enrollment in the last five years: 1986–1987

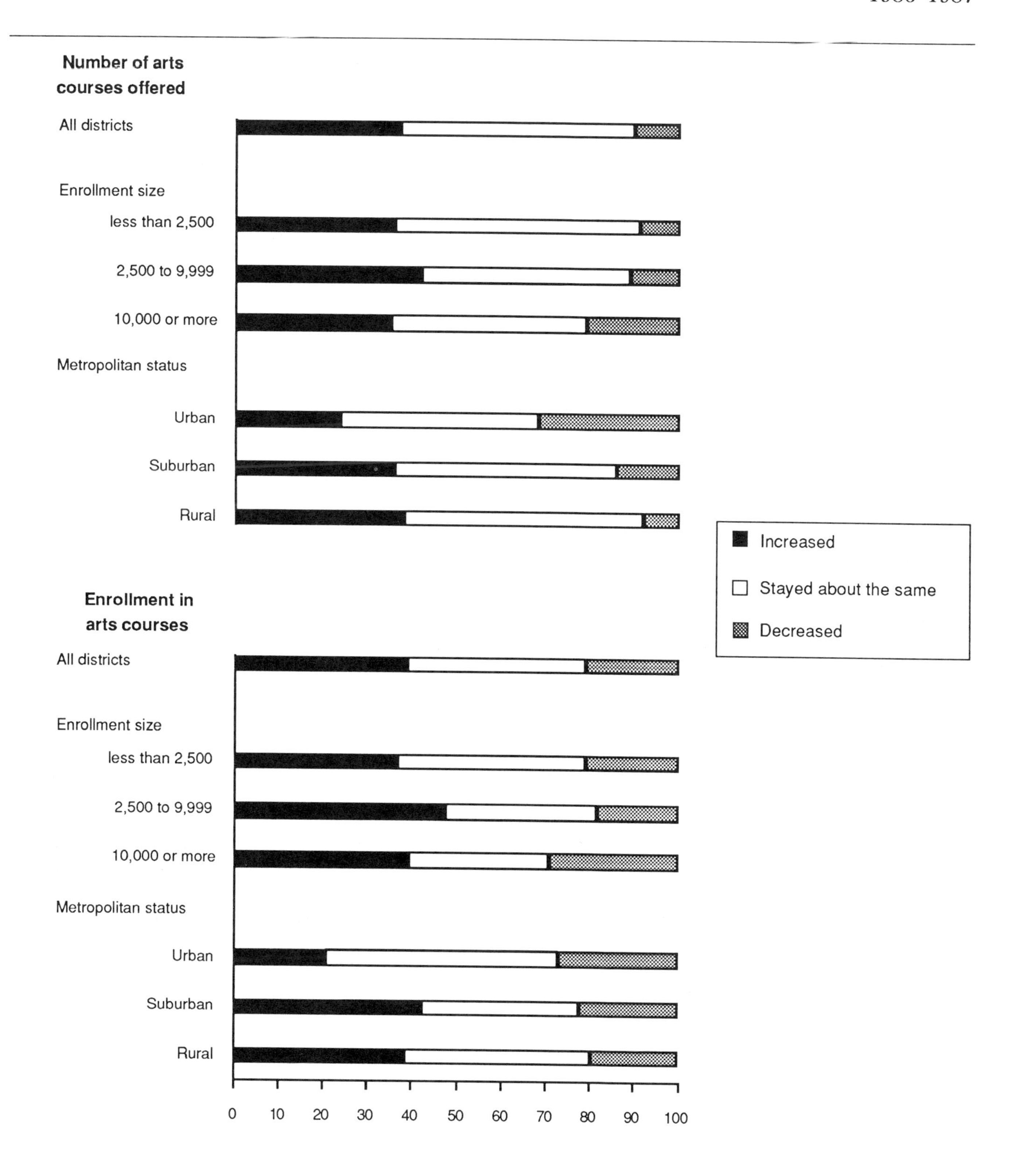

5.7 Enrollments by size and metropolitan status

Students enrolled in courses or participating in programs in selected subjects, by enrollment size and metropolitan status: 1986–1987

	Mean percentage of students enrolled or participating in programs						
		Enrollment size			Metropolitan status		
Subject and grade	**All districts**	**Less than 2,500**	**2,500 to 9,999**	**10,000 or more**	**Urban**	**Suburban**	**Rural**
Music (general)							
Grades 7–8	48	54	51	42	54	42	52
Grades 9–10	12	14	14	10	13	8	17
Grades 11–12	9	11	11	8	9	7	13
Instrumental music							
Grades 7–8	23	29	22	20	21	23	24
Grades 9–10	16	20	15	14	13	15	18
Grades 11–12	14	18	14	13	11	14	16
Choral music							
Grades 7–8	23	31	23	18	17	22	26
Grades 9–10	13	16	13	12	9	12	15
Grades 11–12	12	14	11	11	8	12	13
Visual arts							
Grades 7–8	53	61	53	49	58	52	51
Grades 9–10	21	18	19	22	22	22	17
Grades 11–12	16	15	15	18	15	19	13
Other arts							
Grades 7–8	14	17	13	13	14	14	13
Grades 9–10	12	12	12	13	12	12	12
Grades 11–12	13	12	11	13	12	13	12
Foreign language							
Grades 7–8	21	16	23	22	24	24	16
Grades 9–10	30	27	31	31	27	36	25
Grades 11–12	23	21	25	23	19	27	20

Note: Data in this table have been weighted to reflect the estimated total number of students at the applicable grades. This was done by multiplying the district weight by an estimate of the total enrollment at the applicable grades. The estimation assumed equal distribution of enrollment throughout the grades covered by the district.

Source: Public School District Policies and Practices in Selected Aspects of Arts and Humanities Instruction (Washington, DC: U.S. Department of Education Center for Education Statistics), p. 22.

Students enrolled in courses or participating in programs on selected subjects: 1986–1987

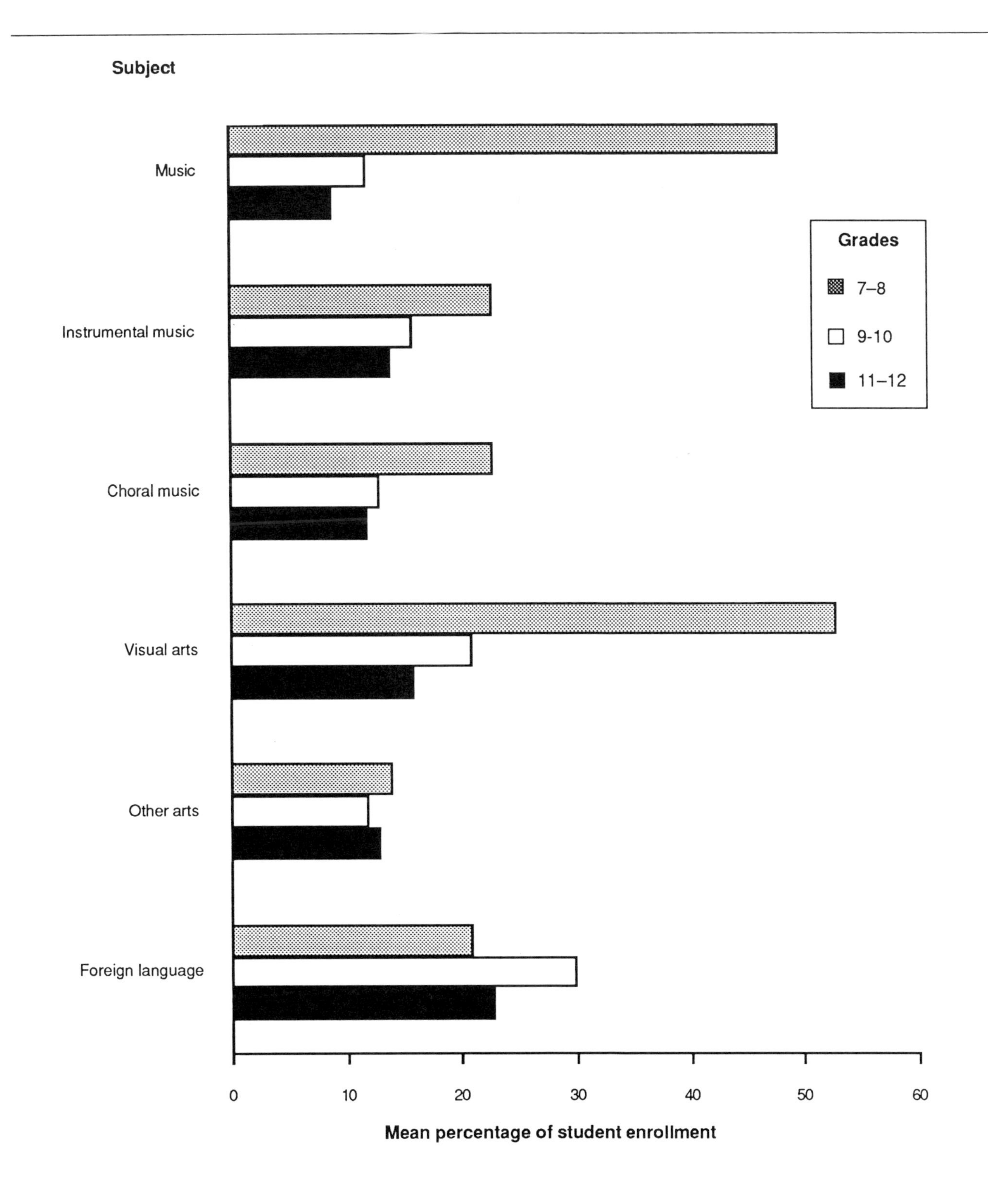

5.8 Extracurricular activities

Participation of high school seniors in extracurricular activities: Spring 1982

	Seniors participating in activities (%)											
Students and school characteristics	Any extracurricular activity	Varsity athletic teams	Vocational education clubs	**Chorus or dance**	Hobby clubs	Subject-matter clubs	Newspaper, magazine, or yearbook clubs	Honorary clubs	Student council, government, political clubs	**Band or orchestra**	Cheerleaders, pep clubs, majorettes	**Debating or drama**
All 1982 seniors	79	36	24	20	20	20	18	16	16	14	14	13
Grade-point average[a]												
3.51 to 4.00	96	42	20	24	16	37	33	75	31	23	21	19
3.01 to 3.50	88	40	22	21	16	26	24	32	23	19	18	18
2.51 to 3.00	81	35	24	19	20	18	20	7	16	14	13	13
2.01 to 2.50	76	34	27	19	20	17	14	3	12	11	12	11
2.00 or less	68	30	23	18	21	16	9	3	8	9	9	9
Boys, by race/ethnicity												
White	76	44	19	10	23	15	14	13	13	12	4	11
Black	79	55	24	18	24	22	12	11	15	17	4	12
Hispanic	76	46	25	12	27	18	12	8	13	12	6	11
Asian	73	41	5	8	29	26	13	28	15	11	3	6
Native American	75	33	39	9	37	17	10	11	10	28	3	9
Girls, by race/ethnicity												
White	83	26	25	27	16	24	25	21	19	16	23	16
Black	82	25	35	36	16	26	20	14	24	15	27	15
Hispanic	77	23	31	27	18	27	19	11	18	13	22	12
Asian	77	22	11	23	19	28	26	32	26	15	12	16
Native American	76	22	28	21	31	16	30	7	12	7	21	9
Socioeconomic status[b]												
Low	75	29	32	18	18	20	15	9	12	10	12	9
Medium	79	35	25	19	21	20	17	14	15	15	15	12
High	85	44	14	22	21	22	25	25	23	16	14	19
Curriculum												
Academic	87	45	14	23	20	25	25	26	24	17	15	17
General	72	32	22	19	21	16	16	7	11	13	13	12
Vocational	74	26	39	16	20	18	12	7	10	11	12	8
School size[c]												
Small	87	45	30	23	19	22	29	18	20	17	19	17
Medium	77	33	22	18	20	21	15	15	16	13	13	12
Large	73	30	19	17	20	18	13	15	14	12	10	11

[a] Cumulative grade-point averages were calculated by the Center for Education Statistics from high school transcripts collected for a "High School and Beyond" subsample. The average is based on a scale where an A is 4.00, a B is 3.00, a C is 2.00, a D is 1.00, and an F is 0.

[b] Socioeconomic status (SES) was measured by a composite score based on parental education, family income, father's occupation, and household characteristics. Three SES categories were formed: low (bottom quartile), medium (middle two quartiles), and high (top quartile).

[c] Schools were divided by size based on Fall 1981 Grade 12 enrollments reported by schools: small (200 or fewer students), medium (201 to 500 students), and large (more than 500 students).

Source: U.S. Department of Education, Center for Education Statistics, "Extracurricular Activity Participants Outperform Other Students." (This table was prepared October 1986.) As included in the U.S. Department of Education, Center for Education Statistics, *Digest of Education Statistics: 1987*, U.S. Government Printing Office, Washington, DC, May 1987, table 85, p. 98.

5.8a Extracurricular activities

Participation of high school seniors in extracurricular activities: Spring 1982

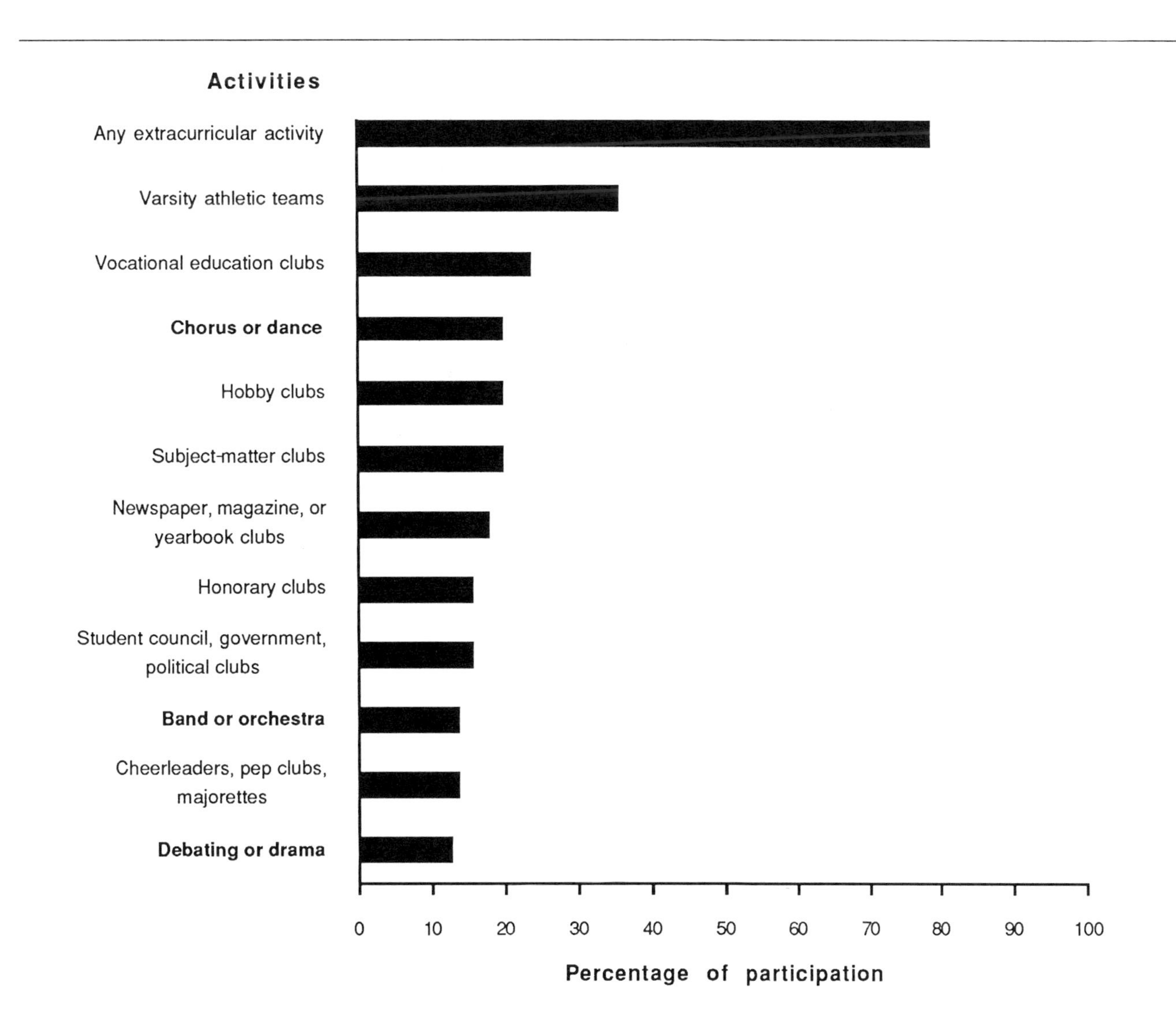

5.9 Enrollments by region

Students enrolled in courses or participating in programs in selected subjects, by geographic region: 1986–1987

Subject and grade	All districts	Northeast	Central	Southeast	West
	Mean percentage of students enrolled or participating				
		Geographic region[a]			
Music (general)					
Grades 7–8	48	81	51	45	21
Grades 9–10	12	21	13	9	7
Grades 11–12	9	15	11	7	5
Instrumental music					
Grades 7–8	23	22	27	17	23
Grades 9–10	16	14	21	13	14
Grades 11–12	14	12	19	12	12
Choral music					
Grades 7–8	23	27	30	16	16
Grades 9–10	13	13	19	9	9
Grades 11–12	12	11	17	9	7
Visual arts					
Grades 7–8	53	79	59	42	35
Grades 9–10	21	28	24	14	16
Grades 11–12	16	18	21	13	14
Other arts					
Grades 7–8	14	12	17	9	15
Grades 9–10	12	10	15	10	13
Grades 11–12	13	12	16	10	11
Foreign language					
Grades 7–8	21	49	20	9	11
Grades 9–10	30	47	29	25	23
Grades 11–12	23	32	22	20	20

[a] See Appendix for states in each geographic region.

Note: Data in this table have been weighted to reflect the estimated total number of students at the applicable grades. This was done by multiplying the district weight by an estimate of the total enrollment at the applicable grades. The estimation assumed equal distribution of enrollment throughout the grades covered by the district.

Source: Public School District Policies and Practices in Selected Aspects of Arts and Humanities Instruction (Washington, DC: U.S. Department of Education Center for Education Statistics), p. 23.

Chapter 6

School District Policies and Practices

Information in this chapter was collected with a single-page questionnaire that was mailed to a sample of United States school districts. Instructions directed the district official completing the form to estimate if exact data were not available.

6.1 District arts resources

Percentage of school districts having selected arts resources: 1986–1987

District policy/ characteristic	Music			Visual arts			Other arts		
	Elementary	Middle/ junior	Senior high	Elementary	Middle/ junior	Senior high	Elementary	Middle/ junior	Senior high
Curriculum guides[a]	75	75	75	67	72	74	35	38	50
Competency tests[b]	6	6	7	6	5	7	4	4	6
Textbook list[c]	54	53	46	37	41	43	23	28	33
Curriculum coordinator[d]	56	56	56	51	52	54	30	35	38

[a] [District] curriculum guides that specify instructional goals in terms of student outcome have been adopted.

[b] Districtwide competency tests [in this subject area] are required for promotion to the next school grade.

[c] A list of recommended or required textbooks has been developed by the district.

[d] A curriculum coordinator or the equivalent directs the program.

Note: The following definitions were used for this study: the visual arts are drawing, painting, sculpture, photography, crafts, and film; music is choral, instrumental, and general; other arts are dance, drama, and creative writing.

Source: Public School District Policies and Practices in Selected Aspects of Arts and Humanities Instruction (Washington, DC: U.S. Department of Education Center for Education Statistics), p. 15.

6.1a District arts resources: Music

Percentage of school districts having selected music resources: 1986–1987

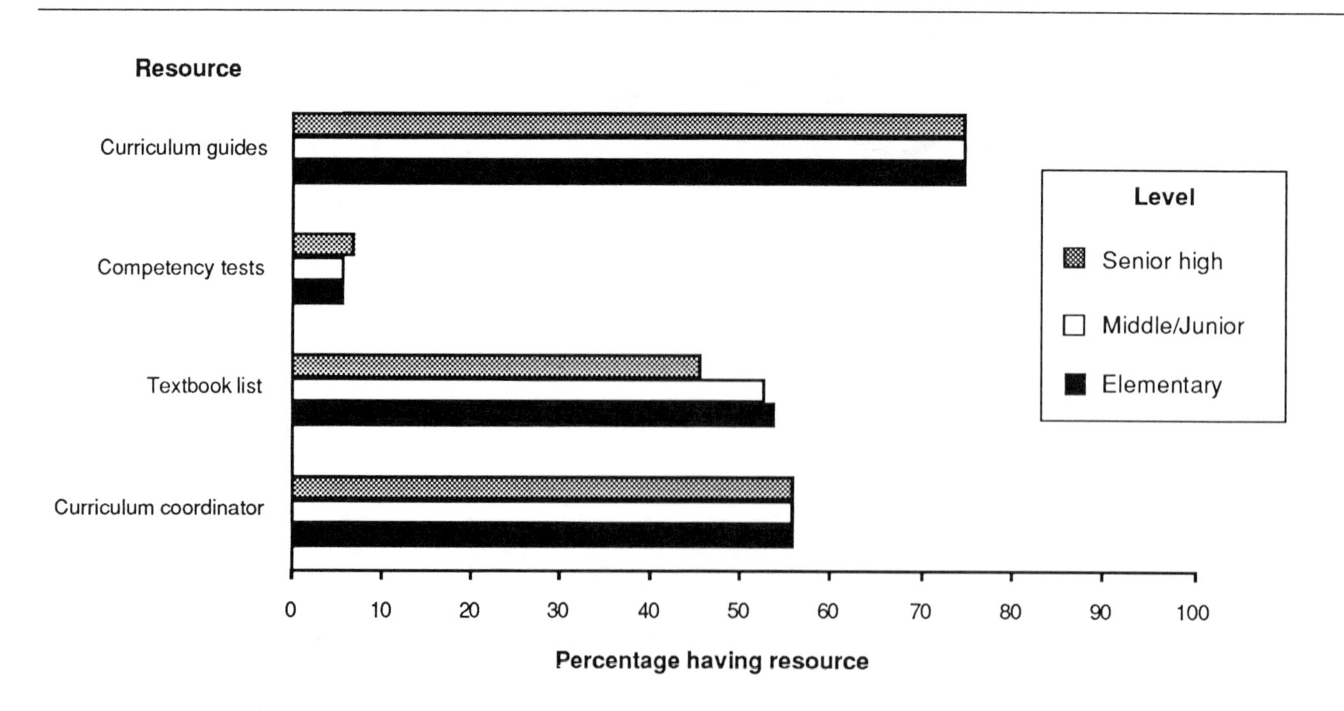

6.1b District arts resources: Visual Arts

Percentage of school districts having selected resources for visual arts: 1986–1987

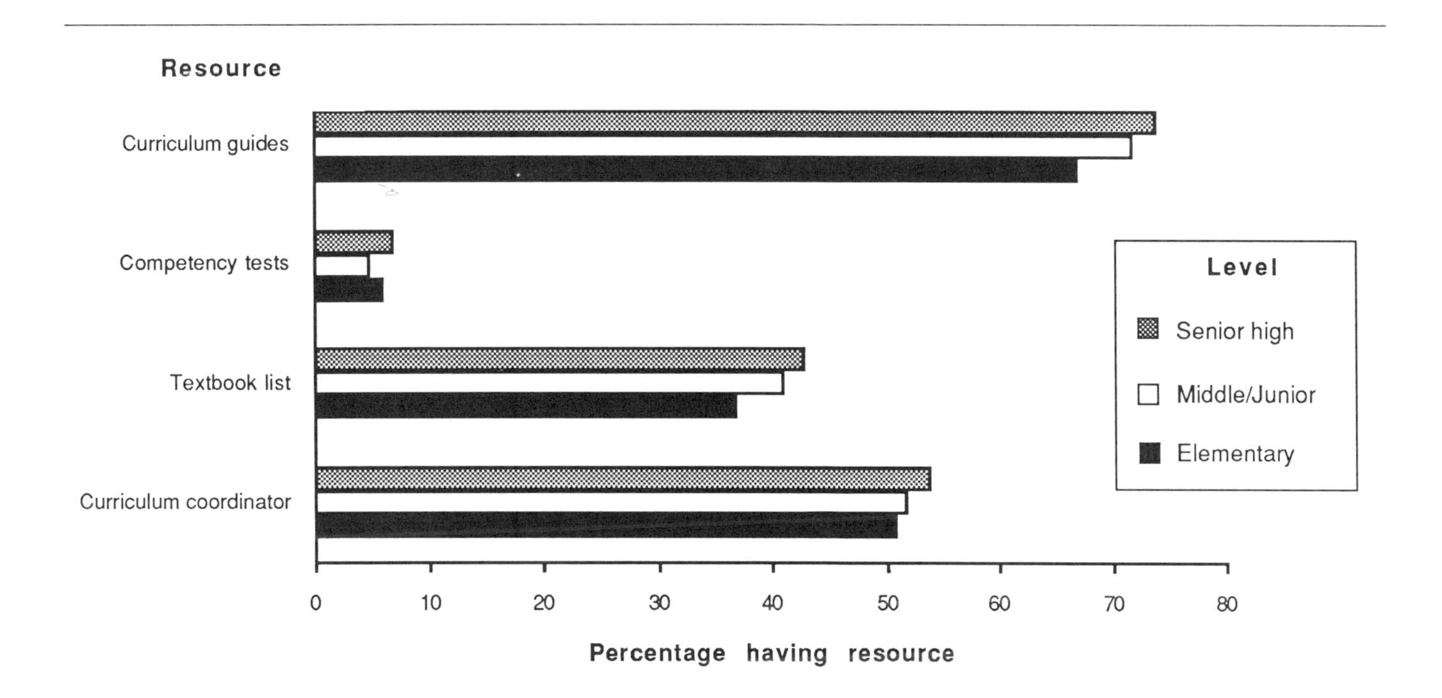

6.1c District arts resources: Other arts

Percentage of school districts having selected resources for other arts: 1986–1987

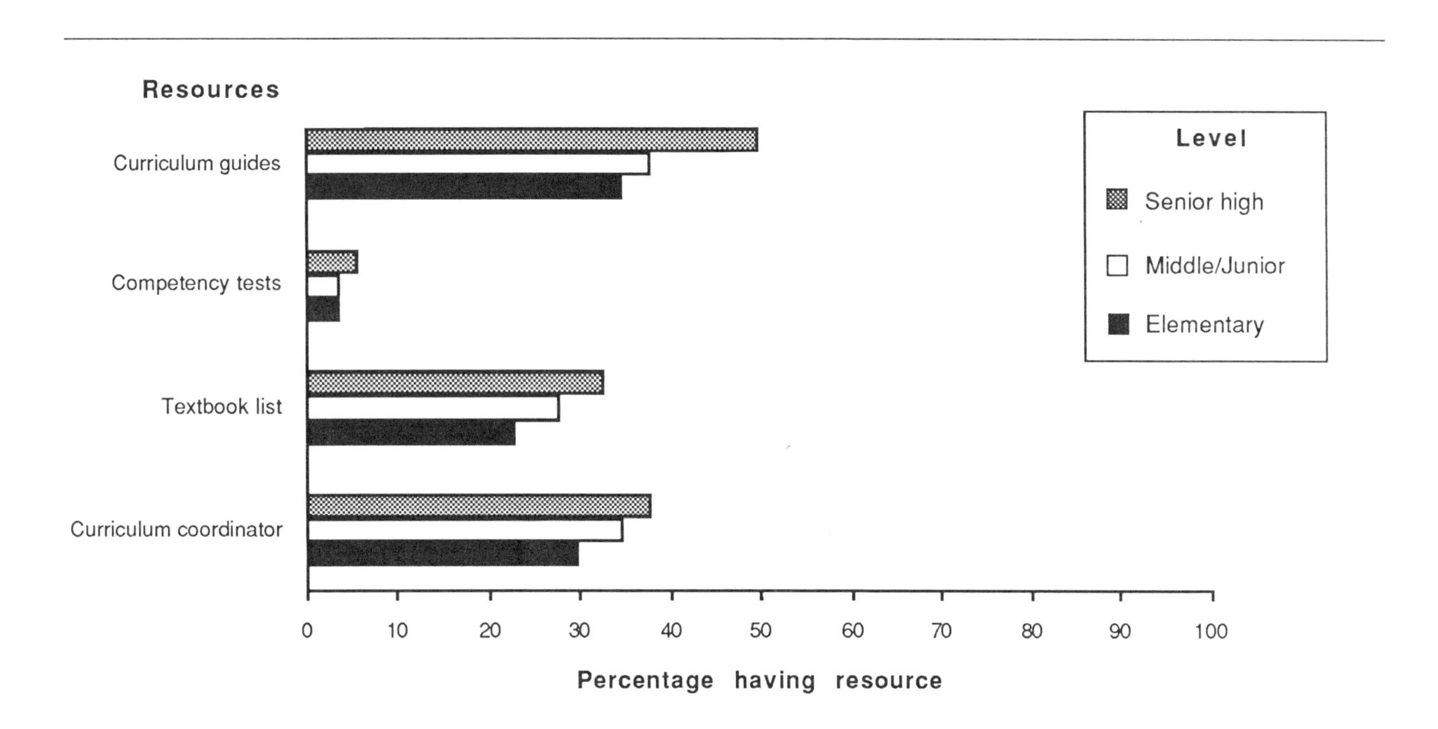

6.2 District arts budgets and time allotments

Changes in district budgets and time allotted to arts education: 1986–1987

		Changes in the last 5 years					
		Percentage of district budget allotted to arts education			Percentage of time allotted to arts instruction at the elementary level		
District characteristic	Total number of districts[a]	Increased	Stayed about the same	Decreased	Increased	Stayed about the same	Decreased
All districts	15,242	50	41	9	34	60	6
Enrollment size							
Less than 2,500	11,506	51	42	8	36	59	6
2,500 to 9,999	2,969	49	41	9	28	65	7
10,000 or more	767	48	32	20	33	58	9
Metropolitan status							
Urban	341	36	45	19	41	48	11
Suburban	4,856	49	38	13	27	64	9
Rural	10,045	51	42	6	37	58	5
Geographic region[b]							
Northeast	3,026	62	33	5	27	67	6
Central	5,945	44	50	6	31	62	7
Southeast	1,709	55	34	11	32	61	7
West	4,562	48	38	14	43	52	5

[a] These numbers reflect the total number of operating districts. Excluded are special, vocational, regional, state districts, and non-operating districts with no enrollment. About 3 percent of the districts do not have any elementary schools, about 25 percent do not have junior high schools, and 19 percent do not have senior high schools. Districts answered questions only for those instructional levels covered within their district. However, those districts providing instruction for grades 7 to 8 in elementary schools answered applicable questions.

[b] See Appendix for states in each geographic region.

Note: Percentages may not total to 100 because of rounding.

Source: Public School District Policies and Practices in Selected Aspects of Arts and Humanities Instruction (Washington, DC: U.S. Department of Education Center for Education Statistics), p. 16.

Changes in district budgets and time alloted to arts education: 1986–1987

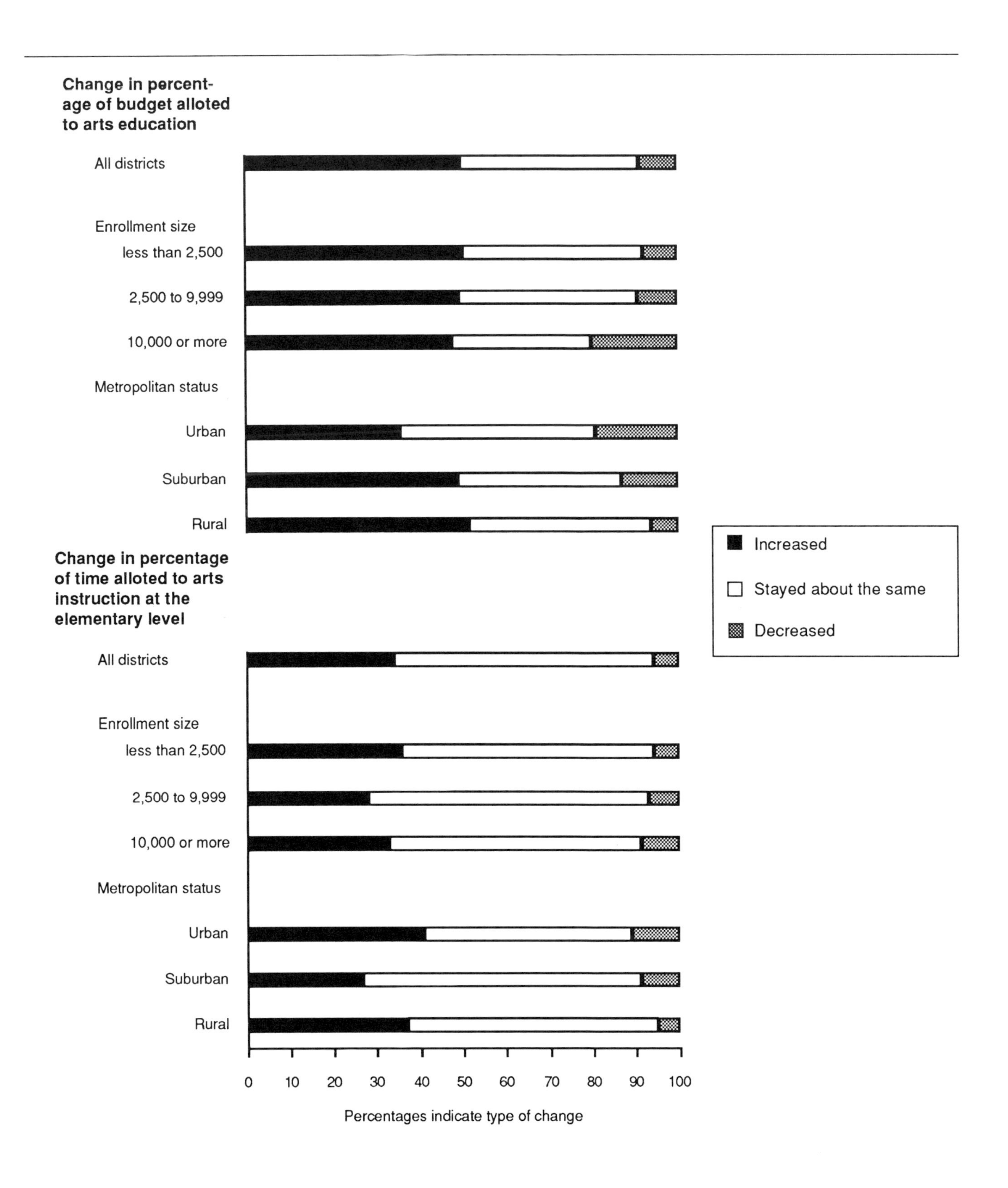

6.3 Total instruction time

Total instruction time devoted to selected subjects: 1986–1987

Subject and grade	Mean minutes per week				Percentage of total instruction time			
		Enrollment size				Enrollment size		
	All districts	Less than 2,500	2,500 to 9,999	10,000 or more	All districts	Less than 2,500	2,500 to 9,999	10,000 or more
Music								
Grades 1–3	76	78	69	73	5	5	4	5
Grades 4–6	84	87	74	77	5	5	5	5
Grades 7–8	134	133	132	148	8	8	8	9
Visual arts								
Grades 1–3	74	76	66	68	5	5	4	4
Grades 4–6	79	80	75	75	5	5	5	5
Grades 7–8	118	114	128	142	7	7	8	9
Other arts								
Grades 1–3	25	26	22	25	2	2	1	2
Grades 4–6	30	31	25	34	2	2	2	2
Grades 7–8	51	49	52	73	2	2	1	2
Social studies								
Grades 1–3	148	151	138	150	9	9	9	9
Grades 4–6	192	194	180	195	12	12	11	12
Grades 7–8	234	233	234	251	14	14	14	15
Language arts/reading								
Grades 1–3	415	394	467	515	25	24	29	34
Grades 4–6	383	368	421	461	23	22	25	30
Grades 7–8	304	299	313	343	18	17	18	21
Total instruction time								
Grades 1–3	1,656	1,669	1,621	1,593	—	—	—	—
Grades 4–6	1,692	1,706	1,655	1,625	—	—	—	—
Grades 7–8	1,736	1,747	1,704	1,693	—	—	—	—

Note: — = Not applicable.

Source: Public School District Policies and Practices in Selected Aspects of Arts and Humanities Instruction (Washington, DC: U.S. Department of Education Center for Education Statistics), p. 20.

Total instruction time devoted to music: 1986–1987

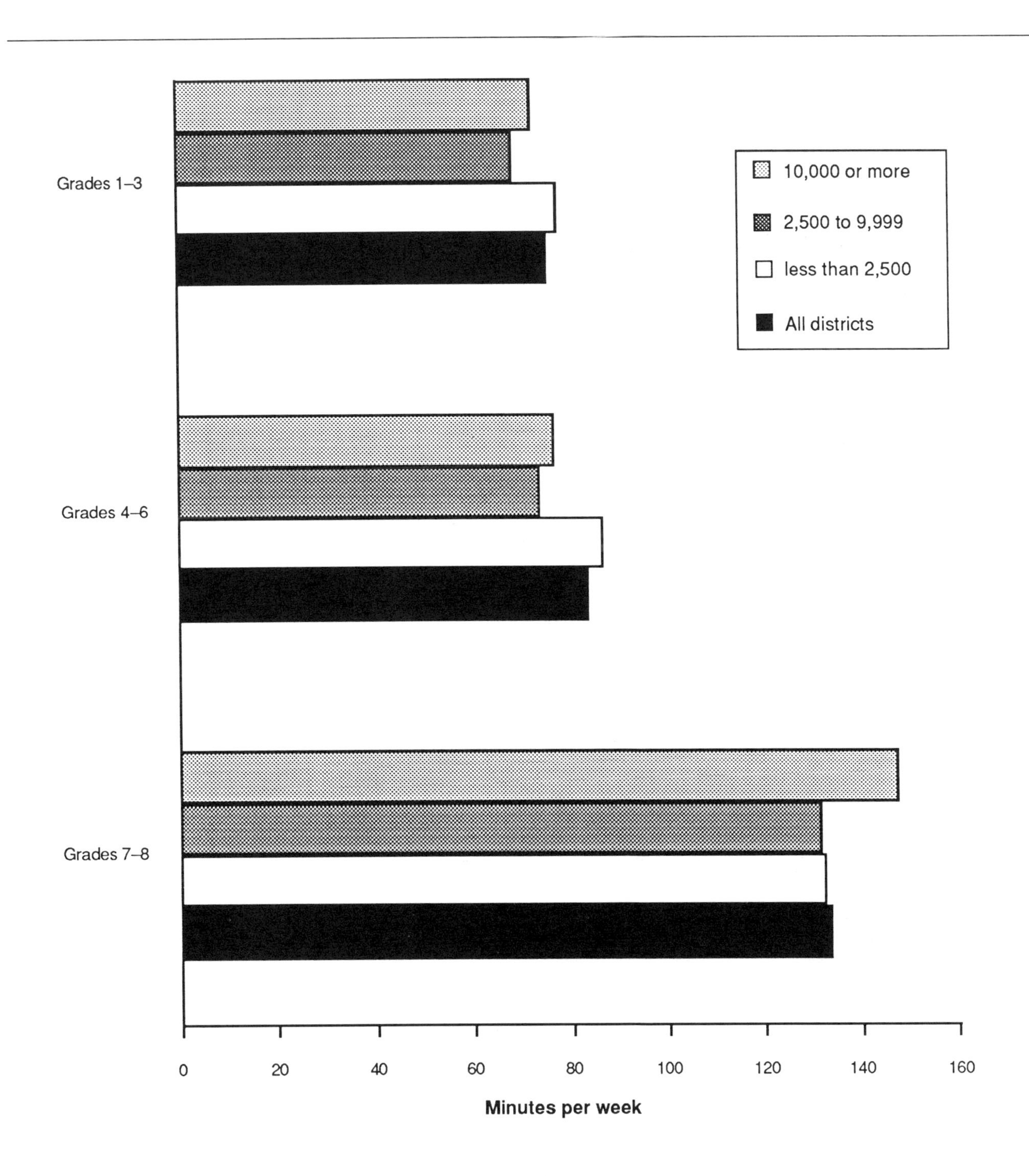

6.3b Total instruction time: Visual arts

Total instruction time devoted to visual arts: 1986–1987

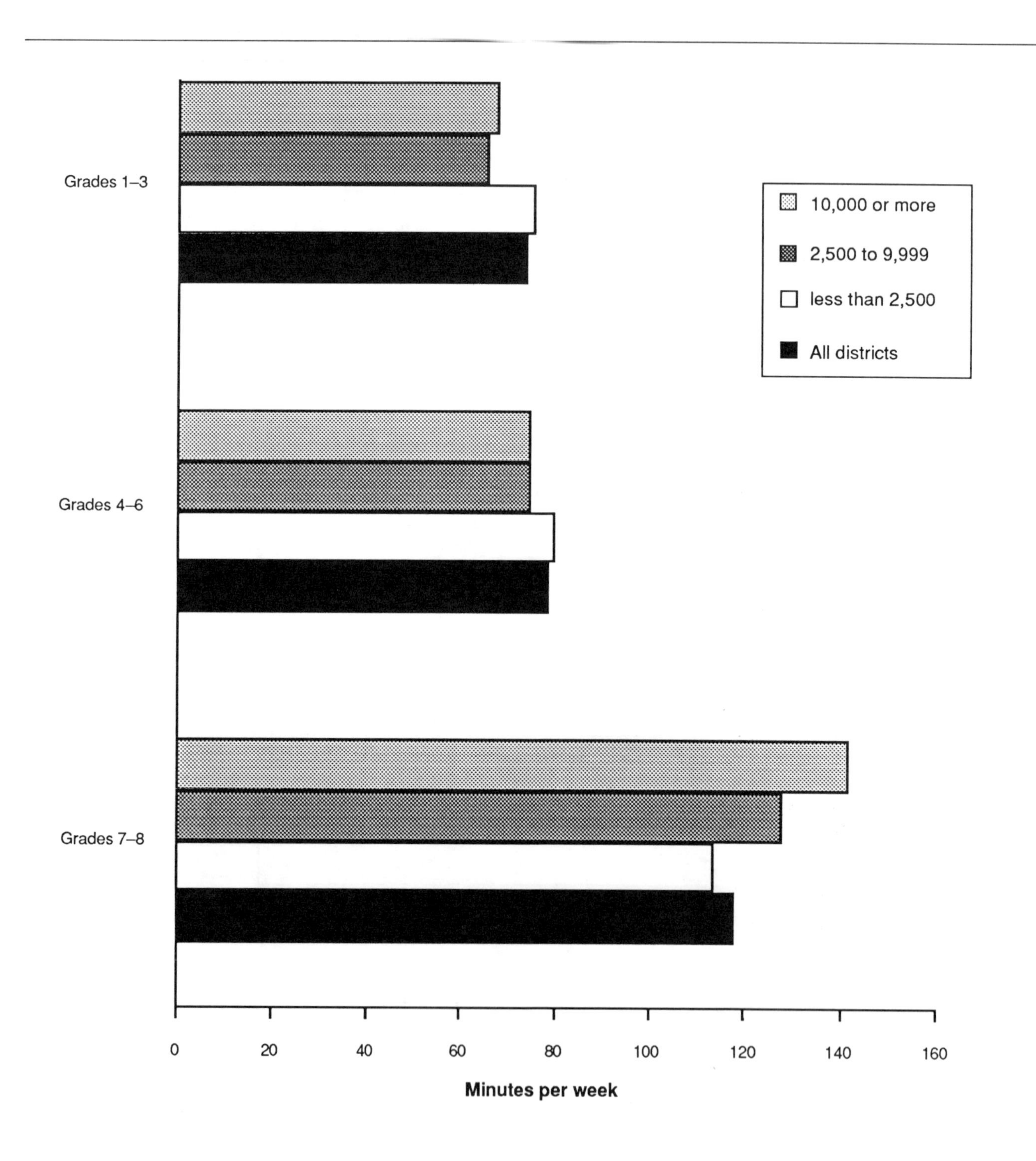

Total instruction time devoted to other arts: 1986–1987

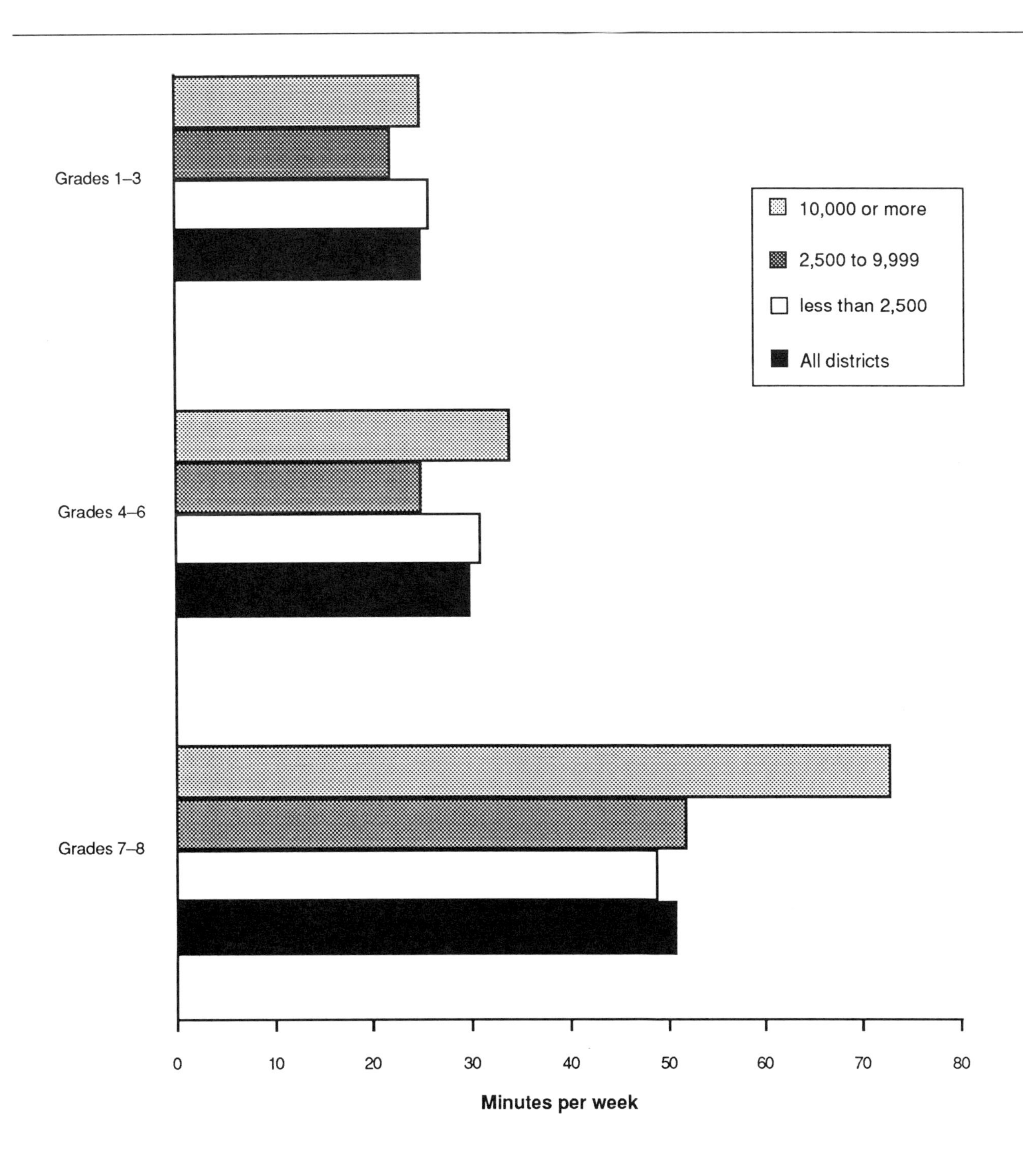

6.4 Elementary arts specialists

Elementary schools in districts served by visual arts and music specialists: 1986–1987

	Percentage of schools served					
	Visual arts specialist			Music specialist		
District characteristic	Served full-time	Served part-time	Not served	Served full-time	Served part-time	Not served
All districts	26	32	42	45	39	16
Enrollment size						
Less than 2,500	22	29	49	43	36	21
2,500 to 9,999	29	37	34	42	44	15
10,000 or more	28	30	42	51	37	12
Metropolitan status						
Urban	32	35	33	39	48	13
Suburban	32	28	40	57	32	11
Rural	19	34	47	37	41	22
Geographic region[a]						
Northeast	50	35	15	60	37	3
Central	26	30	44	46	35	19
Southeast	16	39	44	39	41	20
West	16	26	58	37	42	21

[a] See Appendix for states in each geographic region.

Note: Data in this table have been weighted to reflect the total number of elementary schools. This was done by multiplying the district weight by the total number of elementary schools. Percentages may not total to 100 because of rounding.

Source: Public School District Policies and Practices in Selected Aspects of Arts and Humanities Instruction (Washington, DC: U.S. Department of Education Center for Education Statistics), p. 24.

Percentage of elementary schools in districts served by visual and music specialists: 1986–1987

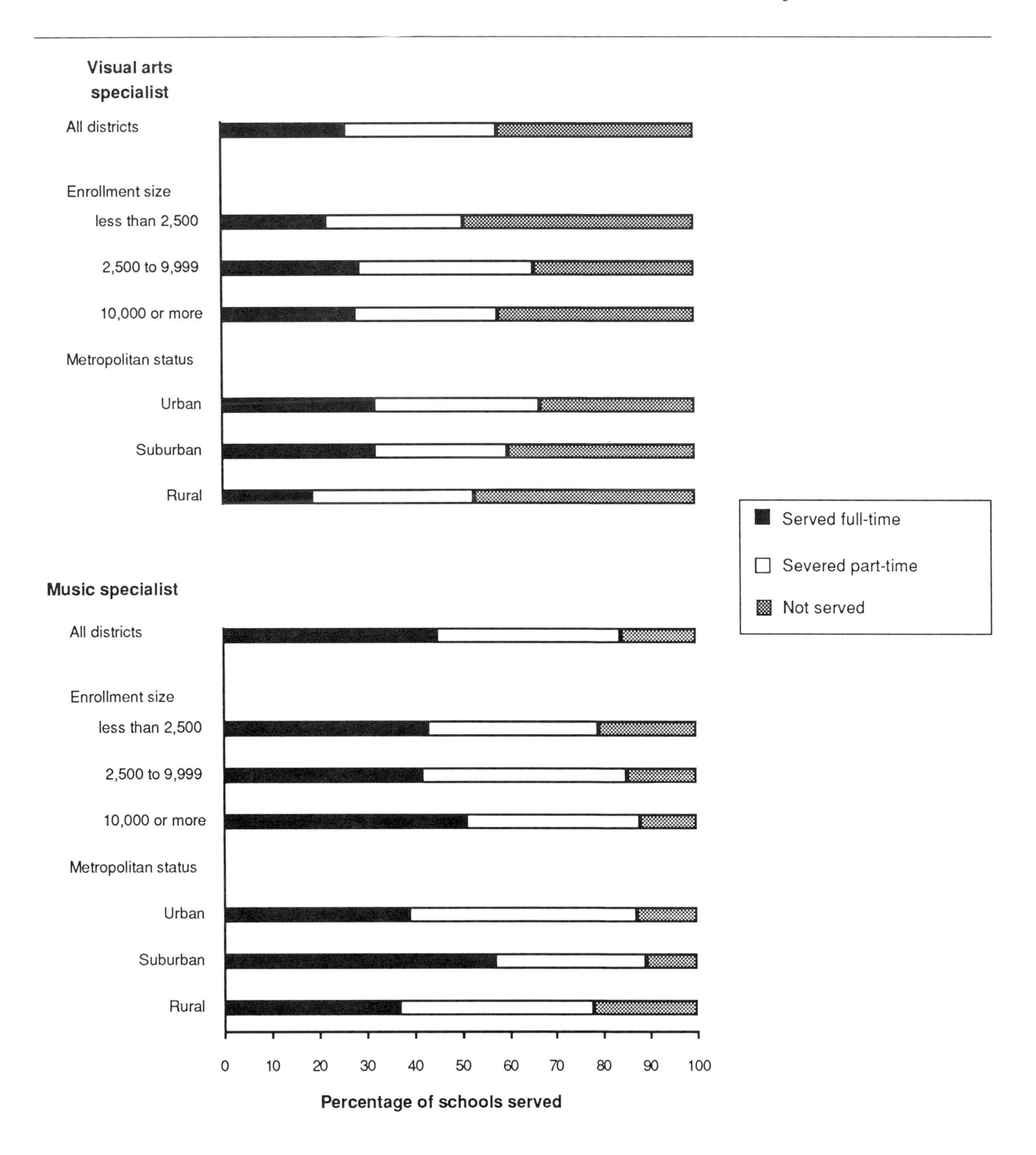

6.5 Graduation requirements by district size

School district graduation requirements by district size: 1981–1982 and 1986–1987

Subject and year graduated from high school	Percentage having credit requirements				Mean number of credits required[a]			
		Enrollment size				Enrollment size		
	All districts	Less than 2,500	2,500 to 9,999	10,000 or more	All districts	Less than 2,500	2,500 to 9,999	10,000 or more
All social studies								
1981–82	100	100	100	100	2.78	2.80	2.79	2.55
1986–87	100	100	100	100	2.98	2.97	3.02	2.85
U.S. history								
1981–82	98	98	97	100	1.04	1.05	1.06	0.98
1986–87	98	98	97	100	1.05	1.05	1.06	0.98
Western civilization/ European history								
1981–82	23	25	19	21	0.21	0.22	0.18	0.18
1986–87	25	25	24	24	0.23	0.23	0.22	0.22
World history								
1981–82	46	48	42	37	0.43	0.45	0.40	0.35
1986–87	52	52	52	52	0.49	0.49	0.49	0.48
American government/ civics								
1981–82	75	75	73	76	0.66	0.65	0.68	0.63
1986–87	80	80	78	86	0.70	0.70	0.71	0.68
Other history								
1981–82	30	30	28	31	0.26	0.26	0.26	0.25
1986–87	34	34	31	41	0.30	0.31	0.29	0.31
Arts (visual arts, music, or other arts)								
1981–82	18	18	19	18	0.19	0.19	0.19	0.17
1986–87	36	35	38	40	0.37	0.36	0.43	0.36
Arts as an option[b]								
1981–82	13	12	14	20	0.17	0.17	0.16	0.29
1986–87	31	26	42	39	0.40	0.35	0.53	0.54

[a] Includes those not having requirements as having "0" credits required.

[b] Arts as an option refers to a requirement in which courses in the arts are an option within a specified group of subjects that fulfill a requirement (e.g., arts or foreign language or computer science).

Source: Public School District Policies and Practices in Selected Aspects of Arts and Humanities Instruction (Washington, DC: U.S. Department of Education Center for Education Statistics), p. 18.

School district graduation requirements in the arts by district size: 1981–1982 and 1986–1987

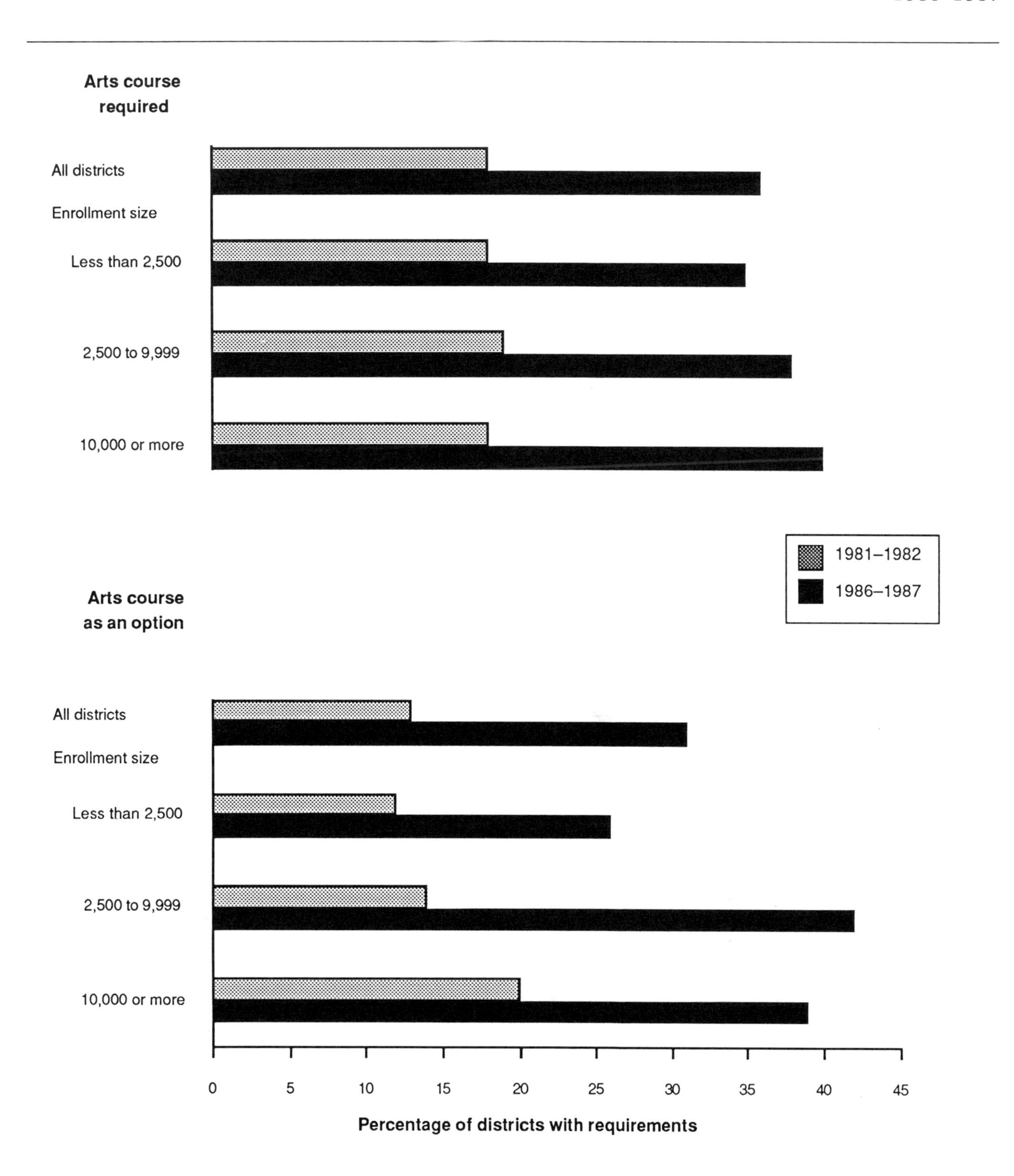

6.5b Graduation requirements by district size

Mean number of arts credits required for graduation by district size: 1981–1982 and 1986–1987

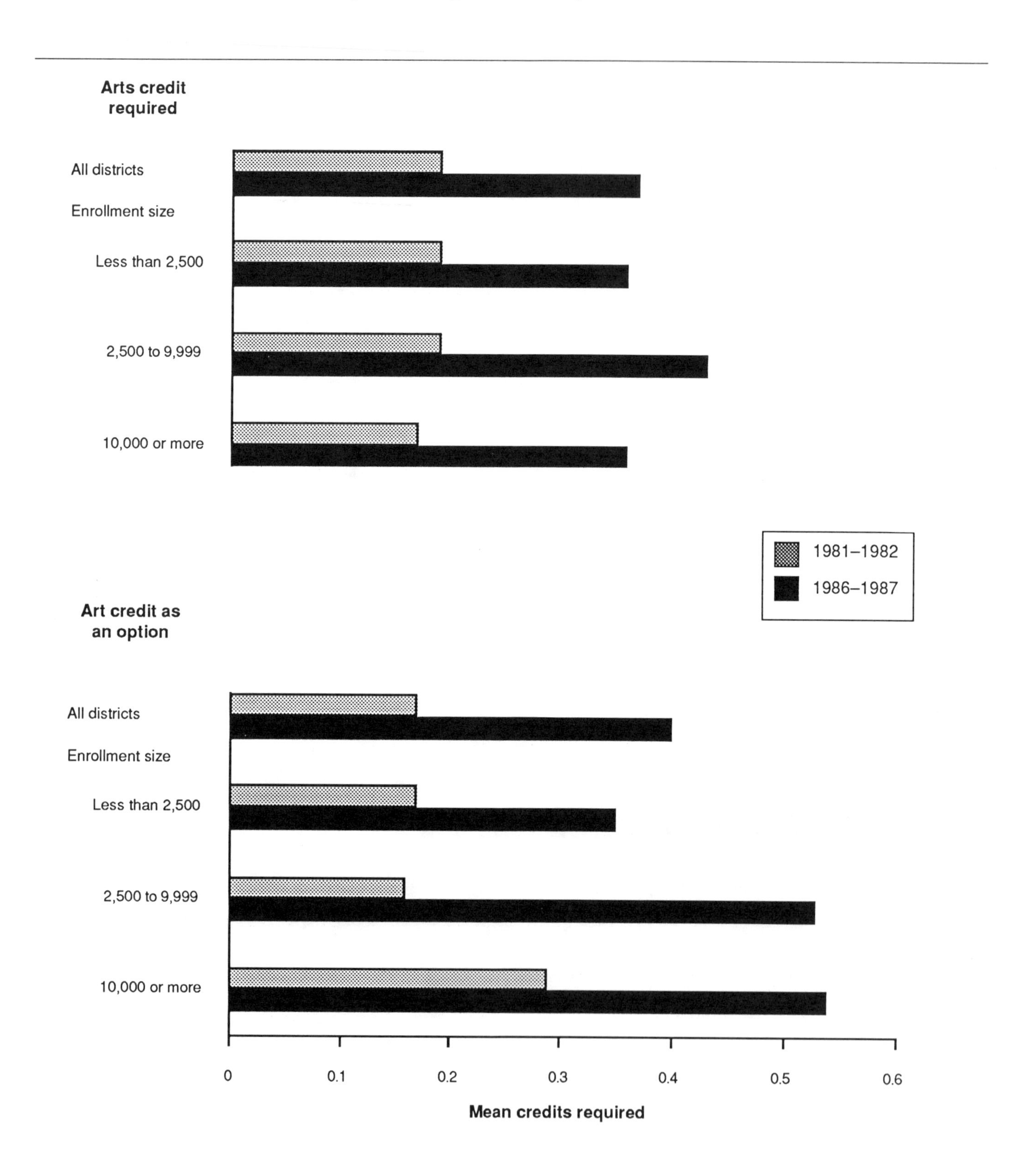

School district graduation requirements by geographic region: 1981–1982 and 1986–1987

Subject and year graduated from high school	Percentage having credit requirements				Mean number of credits required[a]			
	Geographic region[b]				Geographic region			
	Northeast	Central	Southeast	West	Northeast	Central	Southeast	West
All social studies								
1981–82	100	100	100	100	2.89	2.79	2.59	2.78
1986–87	100	100	100	100	3.08	2.98	2.84	2.97
U.S. history								
1981–82	98	98	94	99	1.23	1.05	0.95	1.03
1986–87	97	98	94	99	1.15	1.05	0.94	1.02
Western civilization/ European history								
1981–82	51	19	14	14	0.49	0.15	0.14	0.13
1986–87	54	22	18	12	0.51	0.19	0.17	0.11
World history								
1981–82	40	39	38	66	0.38	0.36	0.37	0.61
1986–87	43	43	48	78	0.41	0.39	0.47	0.71
American government/civics								
1981–82	48	84	71	82	0.45	0.76	0.66	0.65
1986–87	53	89	79	88	0.50	0.79	0.72	0.69
Other history								
1981–82	23	30	32	35	0.24	0.26	0.28	0.26
1986–87	28	35	33	38	0.28	0.31	0.36	0.28
Arts (visual arts, music, or other arts)								
1981–82	29	18	9	15	0.28	0.19	0.09	0.17
1986–87	60	26	29	37	0.66	0.27	0.22	0.41
Arts as an option[c]								
1981–82	17	10	12	15	0.25	0.12	0.16	0.22
1986–87	40	20	31	40	0.53	0.26	0.38	0.53

[a] Includes those not having requirements as having "0" credits required.

[b] See Appendix for states in each geographic region.

[c] Arts as an option refers to a requirement in which courses in the arts are an option within a specified group of subjects that fulfill a requirement (e.g., arts or foreign language or computer science).

Source: Public School District Policies and Practices in Selected Aspects of Arts and Humanities Instruction (Washington, DC: U.S. Department of Education Center for Education Statistics), p. 19.

6.6a Graduation requirements by geographic region

School district graduation requirements in the arts by geographic region: 1981–1982 and 1986–1987

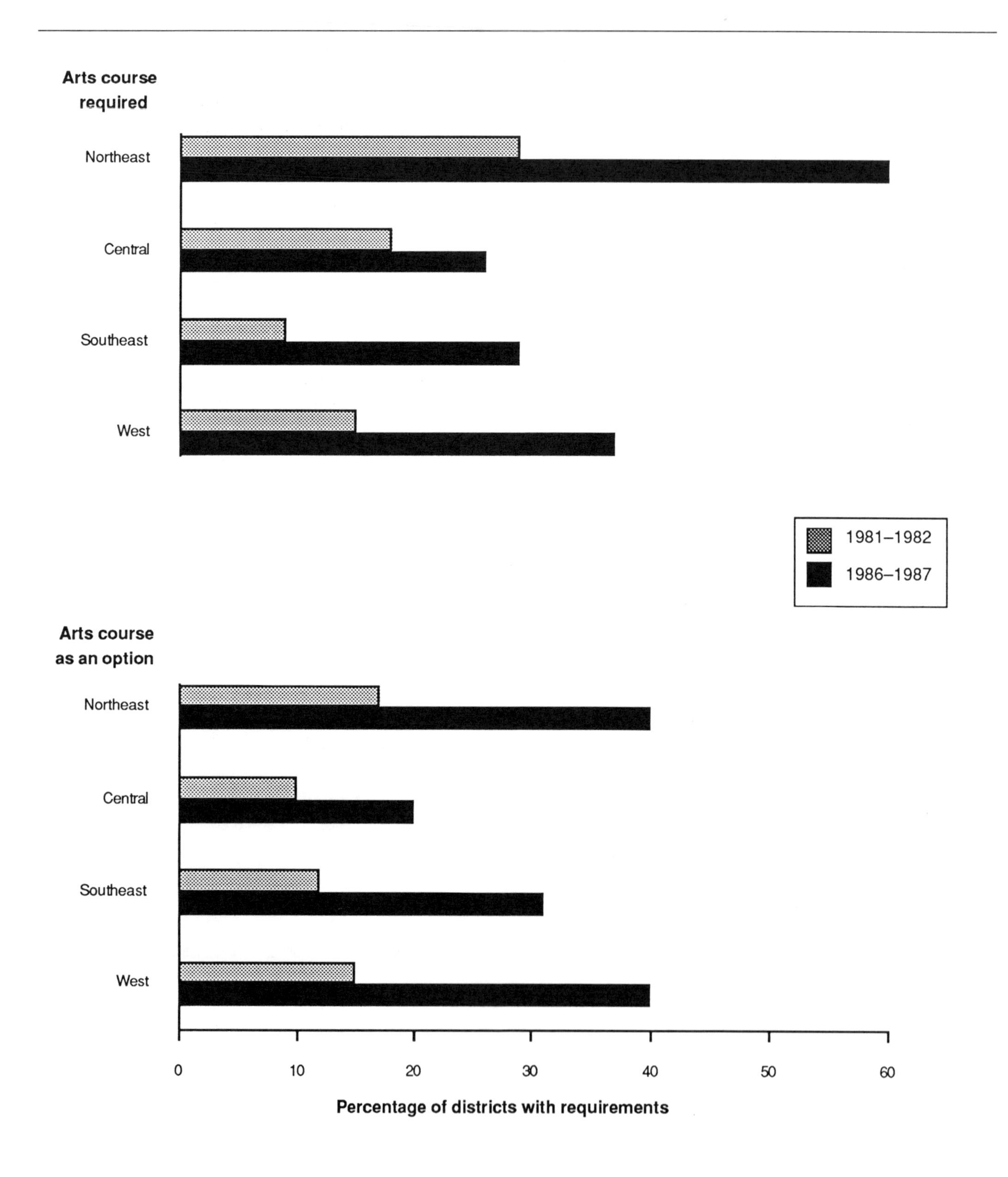

Mean number of arts credits required for graduation by geographic region: 1981–1982 and 1986–1987

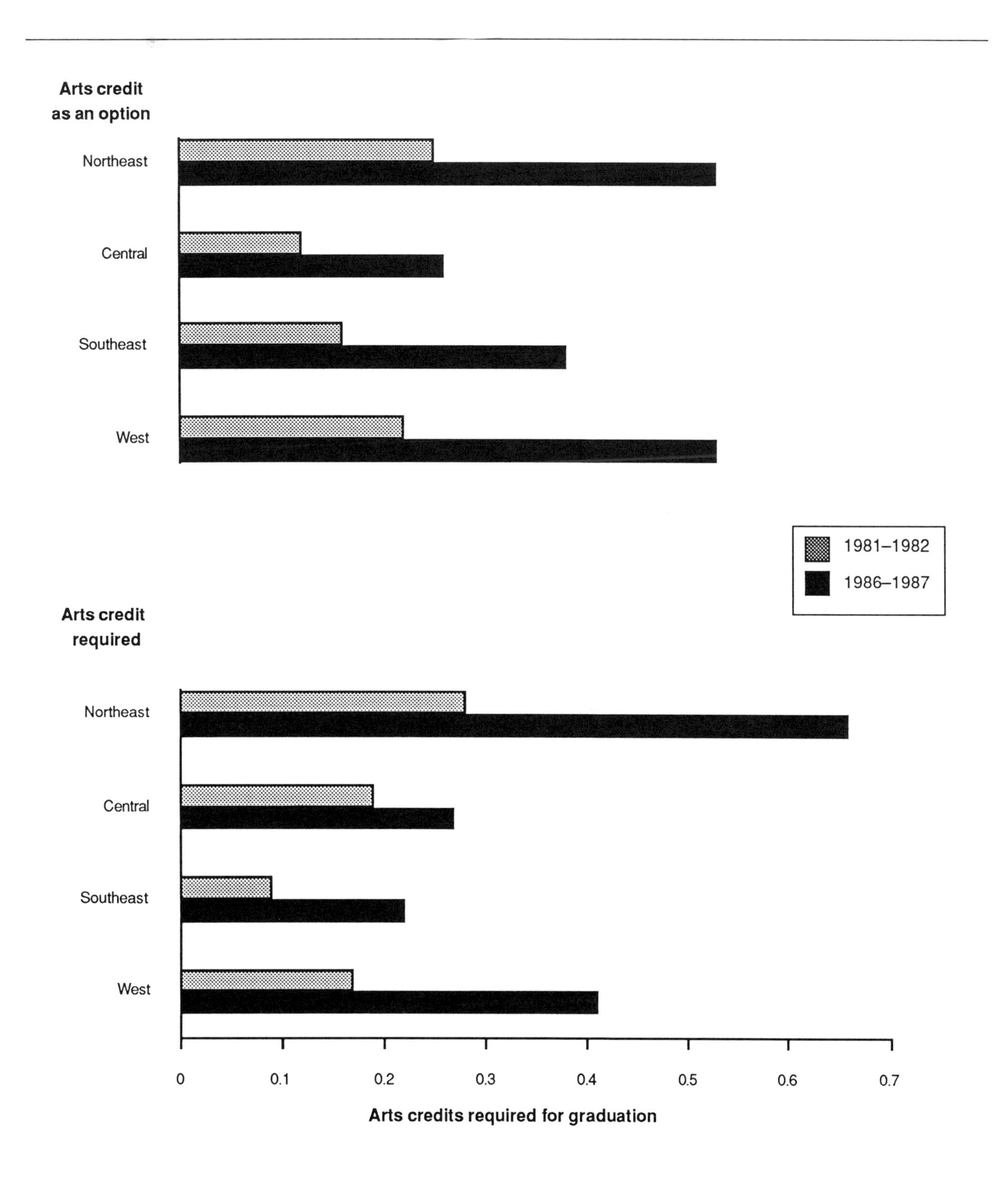

Appendix

This appendix provides information about the data in this book: the names of the organization that reported them, the method of data collection (sample surveys, universe surveys, and compilations of administrative records); the type, size, and constituency of the population used in collecting data; and frequency of the data collecting. This information is provided to assist the reader in understanding the figures presented in the tables. The information presented may clarify what seem to be discrepancies between tables; for example, the teacher shortage reports from the Association for School, College, and University Staff and from the National Center for Education Statistics are different because one requests opinions and the other asks about specific shortages.

Organizations publishing reports are listed alphabetically. Information for a specific report will be found alphabetically under the name of the issuing organization.

U.S. Department of Education, Office of Research

The Standardized Test Scores of College Graduates, 1964–1982

The Graduate Record Examinations (GRE) consist of a general test containing seven 30-minute sections and 15 subject-area tests, each lasting two hours and fifty minutes. The GRE is administered by Educational Testing Service of Princeton, New Jersey. The GRE policies are established by the Graduate Records Examinations Board, an independent board.

GRE test-takers are largely self-selected. Most take the test because they plan to attend graduate schools that require or recommend one or more of the GRE tests as part of the admissions application. Because of self-selection, the scores do not reflect the overall quality of undergraduate education in the United States.

Standard deviation units are used for this analysis because no two GRE examinations have the same scales, and reporting the data in standard deviation units accounts for the different ranges in scores among the many groups of students who took these examinations over a long period.

"Standard deviation unit differences for this indicator were calculated using the following steps: (1) averaging the standard deviations for each test for each of the years in the periods (e.g., 1976–77 through 1986–87); (2) calculating the difference in the mean GRE subtest score for the first and last years of the period (e.g., mean verbal score for the 1986–87 minus mean verbal score for 1976–77); and (3) dividing the difference in the mean score over the period by the average standard deviation over the period to obtain the difference score in standard deviation units." This information is from *1988 Education Indicators*, U.S. Department of Education, Office of Educational Research and Improvement, National Center for Education Statistics, Washington, DC, September 1988, Joyce D. Stern (editor) and Marjorie O. Chandles (associate editor), pp. 252–3.

For more information about this report contact Clifford Adelman, Office of Research, Office of Educational Research and Improvement, U.S. Department of Education, 555 New Jersey Avenue, NW, Washington, DC 20208.

For more information on the GRE contact Graduate Record Examinations, P.O. Box 6000, Princeton, NJ 08541-6000.

Association for School, College and University Staffing, Inc.

Teacher Supply and Demand in the United States: 1989 Report

The Association for School, College and University Staffing, Inc. (ASCUS) is an organization of college teacher placement offices. Since 1976, ASCUS has conducted a yearly opinion survey of its members to gather information about elementary and secondary teacher supply and demand in the United States. In 1976, 1986, 1988, and 1989, surveys were mailed to all members. In other years, the survey used a sample of its members. The basic portions of the survey instrument, including teacher supply and demand, have remained relatively constant, allowing comparative information to be presented. The 1989 survey was mailed to all 521 member placement offices in October 1988. Two hundred ninety-two questionnaires (56 percent) were returned with usable information. This is a typical response rate for these surveys.

The region classifications are as follows: "Northeast" includes Connecticut, Maine, Massachusetts, New Hampshire, Rhode Island, Vermont; "Middle Atlantic" includes Delaware, District of Columbia, Maryland, New Jersey, New York, Pennsylvania; "Great Lakes" includes Illinois, Indiana, Michigan, Ohio, Wisconsin; "Southeast" includes Alabama, Florida, Georgia, Kentucky, Mississippi, North Carolina, South Carolina, Tennessee, Virginia, West Virginia; "South Central" includes Arkansas, Louisiana, Oklahoma, Texas; "Great Plains/Midwest" includes Iowa, Kansas, Minnesota, Missouri, Nebraska, North Dakota, South Dakota; "Rocky Mountain" includes Colorado, Montana, New Mexico, Wyoming; "West" includes Arizona, California, Nevada, Utah; and "Northwest" includes Idaho, Oregon, and Washington.

Copies of the 1989 report are available for $10.00 from the Association for School, College and University Staffing, Inc., 1600 Dodge S-330 Evanston, IL 60201-3451, telephone 708-864-1999. The author of this survey report series is James Akin, Associate Director, Career Planning and Placement, Kansas State University, Manhattan, KS 66056.

Census Bureau

Secondary School Enrollment

While this report is taken from a Census Bureau publication, the original source is a U.S. Office of Education report, *Biennial Survey of Education in the United States, 1948–1950.* These biennial reports were based on forms completed by state departments of education. Since data were collected from all states, no sampling error was introduced. The major factor affecting the accuracy of these figures is the uniformity with which all state units use standard terms, definitions, and procedures.

The original source table included information for 1955, 1959, 1963, and 1965. These years were not included on table 5.1 in this publication because no information was available in those years for music or art. The next available data for music or art are for 1972–73 and can be found in tables 5.2, 5.3, and 5.4.

For more information contact George H. Brown, Elementary and Secondary Education Statistics Division, National Center for Education Statistics, 555 New Jersey Avenue, NW, Washington, DC 20208-5652.

Center for Education Statistics

See National Center for Education Statistics

Center for Statistics

See National Center for Education Statistics

The College Board

The Scholastic Aptitude Test (SAT)

Conducted by the Educational Testing Service (ETS), the SAT is a 2.5-hour, multiple-choice test of students' verbal and mathematical reasoning abilities. Students' scores are reported on a scale of 200 to 800. These scores are intended to supplement the students' secondary school record and other information to assist in predicting academic performance in college.

Students registering for the SAT are asked to complete a Student Descriptive Questionnaire (SDQ). The SDQ contains questions about the student's background, academic record, extracurricular activities, and plans for college study. Because of the 95 percent response rate on the SDQ, ETS considers the data gathered by the SDQ to be a nearly complete and accurate description of the tested population. While large numbers of students take the SAT, test takers are self-selected and do not include all high school graduates nor all students who enroll in colleges and universities. Therefore, SAT reports are only partially representative of high school graduates.

For further information contact The College Board, 888 Seventh Avenue, New York, NY 10106 or College Entrance Examination Board, Educational Testing Service, Princeton, NJ 08541.

National Center for Education Statistics

Between 1985 and 1988 the National Center for Education Statistics underwent several name changes—from National Center of Education Statistics (NCES) to Center for Statistics (CS) to Center for Education Statistics (CES) and finally returning to National Center for Education Statistics (NCES). In this appendix, CES and CS reports are listed under NCES and include the current NCES contact name and address for additional information. Elsewhere in this book, the NCES title that appears on the individual source report is used.

The National Center for Education Statistics (NCES) has federal authorization "to collect, and analyze, and disseminate statistics and other data related to education in the United States and other nations." Currently part of the U.S. Department of Education, it was formerly part of the U.S. Department of Health, Education, and Welfare Office of Education.

Earned Degrees Conferred

Data on earned degrees come from a number of sources. Beginning with the 1986–87 figures, data were gathered with the "Completions" survey of the Integrated Postsecondary Education Data System (IPEDS). The IPEDS surveys all postsecondary institutions, including universities and colleges, as well as a sample of institutions offering technical and vocational education beyond the high school level. The IPEDS consists of several integrated components including the "Completions" survey.

For figures from 1966–67 through 1985–86, data were gathered with the "Degrees and Other Formal Awards Conferred" survey, part of the "Higher Education General Information Survey" (HEGIS). The HEGIS, being replaced by IPEDS, is an annual survey of institutions listed in the latest NCES *Education Directory, Colleges and Universities.* Degree classification taxonomy was revised in 1970–71 and 1982–83.

Figures prior to 1966–67 were collected using the "Survey of Earned Degrees Conferred," mailed separately to colleges and universities. Data of this type were first collected in 1947. Several changes in the taxonomy occurred between 1947 and 1966.

The various changes in taxonomy were made to reflect the changes in both the titles and the general increase in the number of unique degrees that colleges and universities offered. While data in the tables give general trends over time, care should be taken when comparing specific numbers for years with different taxonomies.

For further information on IPEDS contact William Freund, Postsecondary Education Statistics Division, National Center for Education Statistics, 555 New Jersey Avenue, NW, Washington, DC 20208-5652.

Extracurricular Activity Participants Outperform Other Students

This information is based on the first followup, in 1982, of "High School and Beyond," a national longitudinal study of 1980 high school seniors and sophomores. The original 1980 sample was based on a sample of 1,015 schools with a target of 36 seniors and 36 sophomores in each school. This procedure resulted in the selection of 58,270 students who completed a questionnaire and took a battery of cognitive tests. In fall 1982, transcripts were requested for an 18,152-member subsample of the sophomore cohort, resulting in 12,116 usable transcripts in the "High School and Beyond Transcript Survey."

The groupings "chorus or dance," "band or orchestra," and "debating or drama" were used on the questionnaire that students completed. Information cannot be extracted for individual areas, e.g., figures are available only for the combination of chorus or dance—not for chorus only or dance only.

For additional information contact Paula Kneppner, Elementary/Secondary Education Outcomes Division, National Center for Education Statistics, 555 New Jersey Avenue, NW, Washington, DC 20208.

1987 Recent College Graduates Survey

NCES periodically conducts surveys of people about one year after their graduations. The sample is drawn by selecting a sample of colleges and universities that award bachelor's and master's degrees and for each of the selected institutions, choosing a sample of degree recipients. The first of these surveys was conducted in 1976 (of 1974–75 college graduates). It was then repeated in 1981, 1985, and 1987. Tables prepared from the data gathered in these surveys present data for only those occupations listed by at least three percent of the graduates. Therefore, the occupation classifications used vary with the year of the report, and comparison between reports is difficult. For that reason only the most recent data are included in this publication. Data for previous Recent College Graduate Surveys are available from the NCES.

For the 1987 survey, data were gathered from a sample of graduates who received bachelor's or master's degrees from American colleges or universities between July 1, 1985 and June 30, 1986. Data were collected between June 1987 and February 1988. Data about employment experience were for the respondents' status as of April 27, 1987. The questionnaire was sent to a sample of 21,957 graduates and responses were obtained from 16,878 (80 percent) by mail and telephone interview. Nonresponses were primarily because of incorrect or insufficient addresses of graduates.

For further information contact Joanell Porter, Postsecondary Education Statistics Division, National Center for Education Statistics, 555 New Jersey Avenue, NW, Washington, DC 20208-5652.

Teachers in Elementary and Secondary Education

In the school year 1983–84, the Center for Education Statistics conducted a survey to determine the demand for, and availability of, qualified teachers. (This survey was conducted again in 1985 and 1987 but data from those surveys were not available as this publication was compiled.) Survey forms were mailed to administrators in 2,540 of the approximately 15,300 public school systems and to principals and headmasters/mistresses of 1,000 of the approximately 27,000 private schools in the United States. Usable responses were received from 2,263 of the public systems and 809 of the private schools. These responses were weighted and inflated to generate national estimates.

"Head counts" were requested for the number of positions offered and teachers hired for the 1983–84 school year and "full-time equivalent" (FTE) figures were requested on teacher employment, certification, and shortages by specific teaching assignments. The FTE figures were used to calculate national estimates by level and subject. For the teacher shortage portion of the survey, shortages were defined for respondents as "positions vacant, abolished, or transferred to another field...because a candidate was unable to be found."

For further information contact John P. Sietsema, National Center for Education Statistics, 555 New Jersey Avenue, NW, Washington, DC 20208-1401.

A Trend Study of High School Offerings and Enrollments: 1972–73 and 1981–1982

This report is based on three separate surveys: the 1973 "Survey of Public Secondary School Offerings, Enrollments, and Curriculum Practices"; the 1982 "High School and Beyond Course Offerings and Course Enrollments Survey"; and the 1982 "High School and Beyond Transcripts Survey." The 1973 survey sampled public schools with a grade 7 or above. The 1982 survey sampled public and private schools with a grade 12. The analyses for this report used only public schools from the 1982 sample and only schools with a grade 12 from the 1973 sample. Because of the high nonresponse rate on the 1982 course enrollments survey, the 1982 course enrollments figures are based on analysis of the transcript data.

The report cautions the reader to keep in mind that between 1972 and 1982 there was an overall increase of about 14 percent in course-taking behavior. That is, students took about 14 percent more courses during their grade 9 through 12 enrollment. This was, perhaps, because of a tendency of schools to offer more and shorter courses.

For more information contact George H. Brown, Elementary and Secondary Education Statistics Division, National Center for Education Statistics, 555 New Jersey Avenue, NW, Washington, DC 20208-5652.

National Endowment for the Arts

Artists' Employment in 1986

This report is based on the Census Bureau "Current Population Survey" (CPS), a nationwide monthly sample survey of approximately 60,000 households. The CPS deals primarily with labor force data for the civilian noninstitutional population. Employment data are gathered for more than 400 occupations including several artists' occupations. The Census Bureau inflates the weighted sample to provide national estimates. The artist population makes up a small part of the United States population and a correspondingly small part of the CPS sample. This small size limits the statistical reliability of the figures. Data for years prior to 1983 are available but are not directly comparable because of revisions in the occupational categories in 1983.

For further information contact National Endowment for the Arts, Research Division, 1100 Pennsylvania Avenue, NW, Washington, DC 20506. For further information about the Current Population Survey contact the Education and Social Stratification Branch, Population Division, Bureau of the Census, U.S. Department of Commerce, Washington, DC 20233.

National Endowment for the Arts and the National Endowment for the Humanities

Public School District Policies and Practices in Selected Aspects of Arts and Humanities Instruction

Westat, Inc. conducted this survey and prepared the report under contract to the U.S. Department of Education Center for Education Statistics. The questionnaire for this survey was mailed in late May 1987 to a sample of 700 of the approximately 15,250 school districts in the United States. A telephone follow-up was made to nonrespondents in June, and data collection was completed in July. The final response rate was 95 percent. The sample was stratified by enrollment size (less than 2,500; 2,500–9,999; 10,000 or more) and by metropolitan status (urban, suburban, rural). The survey data were weighted to result in national estimates.

The region classifications are as follows: "Northeast" includes Connecticut, Delaware, the District of Columbia, Maine, Maryland, Massachusetts, New Hampshire, New Jersey, New York, Pennsylvania, Rhode Island, and Vermont; "Central" includes Illinois, Indiana, Iowa, Kansas, Michigan, Minnesota, Missouri, Nebraska, North Dakota, Ohio, South Dakota, and Wisconsin; "Southeast" includes Alabama, Arkansas, Florida, Georgia, Kentucky, Louisiana, Mississippi, North Carolina, South Carolina, Tennessee, Virginia, and West Virginia; and "West" includes Alaska, Arizona, California, Colorado, Hawaii, Idaho, Montana, Nevada, New Mexico, Oklahoma, Oregon, Texas, Utah, Washington, and Wyoming.

The questionnaire was mailed to district superintendents with instructions to have the form completed by the person who was most knowledgeable about humanities and the arts in their district. Except for questions about changes over time, responses were requested for the 1986–87 school year. If exact data were not available, respondents were asked to give their best estimates. For the questions pertaining to teacher supply, respondents were requested to mark (+) for a surplus, (-) for shortage, or (0) for a balance between the supply and the demand for teachers for each subject listed.

For additional information contact Elizabeth Faupel, National Center for Education Statistics, 555 New Jersey Avenue, NW, Washington, DC 20208, telephone 202-357-6325.

National Institute of Education

National Assessment of Educational Progress

Since its initiation in 1969, the overall goal of the "National Assessment of Educational Progress" (NAEP) is to determine the educational achievement of students across the United States. Originally designed and conducted by the Education Commission of the States, Educational Testing Service (ETS) of Princeton, New Jersey, began conducting the NAEP in 1984. NAEP is administered yearly to 9-, 13-, and 17-year-olds, and to young adults (ages 25–35). The sample units are stratified by region; within region they are stratified by state and size of community; and for the two smallest sizes of community they are stratified by socioeconomic level. The assessments are administered to individuals or to small groups of students by specially trained personnel.

Assessments in the visual arts were administered in 1974–75 and 1978–79. Music assessments were conducted in 1971–72 and 1978–79. Major changes in the design of the NAEP were made with the change in the administration to the ETS. The new design is explained in detail in *A New Design for a New Era*, available from ETS at the address below. During the examination that occurred with the change in administration, the decision was made not to continue assessments in art and music.

The region classifications are as follows: "Northeast" includes Connecticut, Delaware, the District of Columbia, Maine, Maryland, Massachusetts, New Hampshire, New Jersey, New York, Pennsylvania, Rhode Island, and Vermont; "Central" includes Illinois, Indiana, Iowa, Kansas, Michigan, Minnesota, Missouri, Nebraska, North Dakota, Ohio, South Dakota, and Wisconsin; "Southeast" includes Alabama, Arkansas, Florida, Georgia, Kentucky, Louisiana, Mississippi, North Carolina, South Carolina, Tennessee, Virginia, and West Virginia; and "West" includes Alaska, Arizona, California, Colorado, Hawaii, Idaho, Montana, Nevada, New Mexico, Oklahoma, Oregon, Texas, Utah, Washington, and Wyoming.

For more information contact Eugene Owen, Elementary/Secondary Outcomes Division, National Center for Education Statistics, 555 New Jersey Avenue, NW, Washington, DC 20208-5653 or National Assessment of Educational Progress, Box 2923, Princeton, NJ 08541.

Peterson's Guides

Arts Related Graduate Programs

This table was prepared by counting the United States colleges and universities listed for each graduate arts area in *Peterson's Annual Guides to Graduate Study: Book 1 — Peterson's Guide to Graduate and Professional Programs: An Overview 1990.* The Peterson's Guide is prepared yearly from catalogs and bulletins supplied by colleges and universities.

For more information contact Daniel V. Steinel, Information Service Manager, Music Educators National Conference, 1902 Association Drive, Reston, VA 22091-1597, telephone 703-860-4000.

Index

1036-12-1M-12/90